D0056708

A
PERFECT
GANESH

A
PERFECT
GANESH

by
Terrence McNally

GARDEN CITY, NEW YORK

ISBN: 1-56865-075-2

Photographs of the 1993 Manhattan Theatre Club production by Gerry Goodstein.
Design by Maria Chiarino
Manufactured in the United States of America

A PERFECT GANESH was produced at the Manhattan Theatre Club (Lynne Meadow, Artistic Director; Barry Grove, Managing Director) in New York City, on June 27, 1993. It was directed by John Tillinger; the set design was by Ming Cho Lee; the costume design was by Santo Loquasto; the lighting design was by Stephen Strawbridge; the sound design was by Scott Lehrer; movement direction was by Carmen de Lavallade; the production stage manager was Pamela Singer and the stage manager was Craig Palanker. The cast was as follows:

GANESHA	Dominic Cuskern
MAN	Fisher Stevens
MARGARET CIVIL	Frances Sternhagen
KATHARINE BRYNNE . . .	Zoe Caldwell

THE PLAYERS

MARGARET CIVIL   Handsome, good bearing, not noisy.
KATHARINE BRYNNE   Vivid-looking, forthright, an enthusiast.
MAN   Someone else in each scene.
GANESHA   A Hindu god. He has an elephant's head. His body is
covered in gilt.

THE SETTING

The play takes place during two weeks in India—getting there and
coming home, too.

THE TIME

Now. Or very recently.

For
Don Roos

ACT ONE

ACT ONE

ACT I

Scene One

Silence. The lights come up slowly on a stage which has been painted a blinding white. GANESHA *is there. He is eating fruit and vegetables his followers have left him as offerings. He looks at us.*

GANESHA: I am happy. Consider. I am a son of Shiva. My mother was Parvati. I am a god. My name is Ganesha. I am also called Vighneshwara, the queller of obstacles, but I prefer Ganesha. To this day, before any venture is undertaken, it is Ganesha who is invoked and whose blessings are sought. Once asked, always granted. I am a good god. Cheerful, giving, often smiling, seldom sad. I am everywhere. (*Music.* GANESHA *begins to gently dance*) I am in your mind and in the thoughts you think, in your heart, whether full or broken, in your face and in the very air you breathe. Inhale, *c'est moi*, Ganesha. Exhale, *yo soy*, Ganesha. *Ich bin; io sono. Toujours*, Ganesha! I am in what you eat and what you evacuate. I am sunlight, moonlight, dawn and dusk. I am stool. I am in your kiss. I am in your cancer. I am in the smallest insect that crawls across your picnic blanket towards the potato salad. I am in your hand that squashes it. I am everywhere. I am happy. I am Ganesha. They're coming! (*Music stops.* GANESHA *stops dancing*) I can see them. I can see everything. They're just outside the International Departures terminal, struggling out of Alan's sensible, metallic blue Volvo station wagon. Not a Sky Cap in sight. George is at home in Stamford watching a desultory quarter-finals match in the Virginia Slims Tournament coming live from Tampa on the Sports Channel. George doesn't particularly like women's tennis but he is paralyzed this evening. He didn't even get up when his wife left. Katharine kissed the top of his head while he let his head roll to his right shoulder so that it connected with, lay against, her right hand resting there. But their eyes didn't meet. "Well, I'm off." He'll miss her, he knows that already, but he doesn't know how much. "You sure you have enough money?" He is always asking her that.

(*Lights up on* MAN. *He is* GEORGE)

MAN: You sure you have enough money?

GANESHA: Alan and Margaret tooted once from the driveway. (*An auto-mobile horn sounds off*) "More than enough. Don't forget to water the fichus." She decided not to say anything about the children. "I'll miss you."

MAN: I'll miss you, too.

GANESHA: Two toots this time. (*The automobile horn sounds again, twice this time: short, staccato toots*) The Civils aren't the sort of people you like to keep waiting. "I love you. Bye." And she was gone. (*Lights down on* MAN) She was on her way to India. He would never see her again.

(*Lights up on* MAN. *He is an* AIRLINES TICKET AGENT *now*)

MAN: Air India announces the departure of Flight 87, direct service to Bombay, with an intermediate stop in London. Now boarding, Gate 10.

GANESHA: You have to imagine the terminal more bustling. (*He lightly claps his hands twice. At once, we hear the hubbub of excited travelers' voices*) Every seat is taken this evening. A Boeing 747 filled to capacity. It has been for months. It's the feast of Hali where I come from. (Even gods who are everywhere have to come from somewhere!) Entire families are going home for it. Men, women, children. Lots and lots of children. This is Air India, after all! (*He claps his hands again: we at once hear children crying, yelling, laughing, playing*) Listen to them! How could I not be? Happy, that is. Is there a more joyful sound than children? A more lovely sight than their precious smiles? A sweeter smell than their soiled diapers? *There's* a place to bury one's face and know bliss! But I digress. They're here.

(MARGARET *enters. She has two large pieces of matched luggage. The bags are on wheels and she has no trouble pulling them along behind her. She also has a small, matching flight bag and a sturdy, ample purse*)

MARGARET: Good evening. We're on your flight to Bombay this evening. There's two of us. Business Class. Maharani Class, I think you call it. I believe we already have our boarding passes and seat assignments. (*She hands him the tickets*) I think we have adjoining seats. Mrs. Brynne has a window seat and I'm on the aisle. 15A and 15B. At least that's what we asked for and the travel agent assured us we had. I can't sit anywhere but an aisle seat. I'm claustrophobic. Actually, I hate to fly. No offense. I'm a terrible flyer, but I do it. This *is* the 20th Century. Too bad there's not a nice boat . . . Oops! Ship, ship, ship; I always do that! . . . to India. That should be 15A and 15B in Business Class. Maharani Class! That's really very sexist. Shame on you. Shame on Air India. Is there a problem?

MAN (*head never up from his computer keyboard*): There shouldn't be. What is the name of the party you're traveling with?

MARGARET: A Mrs. Brynne. Mrs. George Brynne. Katharine Brynne. B-R-Y-N-N-E. I left her at the passenger drop-off with my husband. One of her bags flew open. But she's definitely here. We both are.

MAN: Let me try something. (*He types furiously*)

MARGARET: Is the flight very full?

MAN: Not a seat.

MARGARET: That's what I was dreading. And lots and lots of children, all screaming, yelling their lungs out, running up and down the aisles all night! When I was their age I was left at home. I wasn't whizzing about from continent to continent, I can tell you that! The 20th Century! Isn't it grand, though! From here to India in what? How long is this flight? Something like eighteen hours, yes?

MAN: It's closer to forty-eight hours, actually.

MARGARET: What? Forty-eight hours! They told me it was eighteen!

MAN: Just a little joke.

MARGARET: Well, it wasn't very funny.

MAN: Eighteen swift hours.

MARGARET: That's what I thought.

MAN: Unless of course.

MARGARET: Unless of course what?

MAN: Unless of course nothing! I'm sorry. You looked like someone I could have a few laughs with. I'm sorry. I don't exactly have the most exciting job or life of anyone who ever lived. A few laughs on the way to the graveyard, I suppose that's asking too much in this, the *gotterdammerung* of American Civilization.

MARGARET: Is there a problem or not?

MAN: Let's hope not.

MARGARET: If you can't give us aisle seats, I'm not going.

MAN: Who made these arrangements?

MARGARET: Our travel agent. Wanderlust Holidays. They're in the Town and Country Mall in Greenwich. A Mrs. Cairn made the booking, Edith Cairn, like the terrier.

(KATHARINE *enters. She has two large, ill-matched suitcases and an alarming amount of carry-ons: flight bags, a portable computer, a camera and a VCR, and a portable music system*)

KATHARINE: "O for a Muse of fire." If I said it once, I've said it a million times and I'll say it again: "O for a muse of fire" to describe all this. Words fail me. The entire English language fails me. If I feel this way in the terminal, can you imagine what I'm going to be like when we actually hit India?. I'm sorry, but this is all too much for a white woman.

MARGARET: Will you keep your voice down?

KATHARINE: So what's up, doc? What's the story?

MARGARET: We're lost in the computer. Leave it to Edith Cairn. She's your friend. I never liked the woman. Look at me: I'm a wreck. I told this nice young man if I can't have an aisle seat, I'm not going.

KATHARINE: I'm sure we'll be fine, Maggie.

MAN: I've got you on standby, just in case!

KATHARINE: *Gracias. Muchas gracias.*

MAN: *De nada.* Let's try another routing.

(GANESHA *has come up behind the ladies and now waits patiently in line behind them. He is wearing a bowler hat and carries a briefcase and* Times *of London)*

MARGARET: I knew this would happen. A wonderful start to a trip. Tally-ho and bon voyage. (*To* GANESHA)

KATHARINE: We're going to India for two weeks. I told my husband, "Enjoy TNT, AMC and canned tuna fish. I'm out of here."

GANESHA: (*presenting his boarding pass):* Excuse me, but am I in order here?

MAN (*after a quick glance):* Yes, you're fine. Go right aboard. Have a nice flight, Mr. Smith.

GANESHA: Thank you very much.

(GANESHA *departs)*

MARGARET: This is ridiculous. We booked this flight months ago.

MAN: That was your first mistake. Excuse me. (*He makes another public announcement*) Air India announces the departure of Flight 87, direct service to Bombay, with an intermediate stop in London. Now boarding, Gate 10.

MARGARET: Look at you: you're exhausted already. I told you not to take so much.

KATHARINE: I'm not exhausted.

MARGARET: None of that is going under my seat. I'm not going to sit all the way to Bombay with my knees up to my chin because you insisted on bringing all that crap with you. I'm sorry, it's not crap. I'm upset. But I'm not going to be your porter, Kitty. You read all the books: travel light. If they had one common theme, one simple message, it was "travel light."

KATHARINE: Let's not fight, Margaret.

MARGARET: We're not fighting. Do you have your passport?

KATHARINE: It's right here.

MARGARET: He's going to want to see your passport. Get it out. (KATHARINE *starts looking for her passport in one of her travel bags*) Can I give you one travel tip, Kitty? You should always be ready to show your passport. Keep it someplace handy. Someplace where you can get to it quickly, without holding everyone up.

KATHARINE: I'm not holding anybody up, Maggie.

MARGARET: I didn't say you were. It was just a tip. (*To* MAN) How are we doing?

MAN: Have you ever been to Zimbabwe? Just a little joke. We're fine.

MARGARET: That's not your passport, Katharine. That's your international driver's license. *That's* your passport.

KATHARINE: What do I do with it?

MARGARET: Hold on to it.

MAN: Would these reservations be under any other name?

MARGARET: Of course not.

KATHARINE: My maiden name is Mitchell, if that's any help.

MARGARET: Why would I make our reservations under our maiden names, Kitty?

KATHARINE: Hers is Bennett.

MAN (*making another announcement*): This is your final call for Air India's direct service to Bombay via London's Heathrow Airport. Air India's Flight 87, final call. Final boarding, Gate 10. All aboard, please.

MARGARET: Now what exactly is going on here?

MAN: I'm afraid you two ladies have vanished without a trace into the vast netherworld of our computer system.

MARGARET: Is that supposed to be funny, too?

KATHARINE: It's not his fault, Margaret. He didn't do it on purpose.

MARGARET: I want those two seats.

MAN: I can't. They're being occupied by a Mr. and Mrs. D.M. Chandra of Hyderabad.

MARGARET: They're our seats. We booked them months ago. Mr. and Mrs. D.M. Whatever will just have to catch the next flight. Or put them in the back of the plane in Tourist Class.

MAN: We don't call it that. We call it Leper Class. All right, all right, Mrs. Civil! I'll tell you what I will do.

MARGARET: No, I will tell you what I will do if you don't give us those seats.

KATHARINE: Give him a chance, Margaret.

MARGARET: No one is sticking me back in Tourist Class with a lot of noisy children and natives. Some of them looked like peasants. Shepherds. I wouldn't be surprised if there were a few goats aboard.

MAN: That's honest.

MARGARET: I want to see India my way, from a comfortable seat, somewhat at a distance.

KATHARINE: That's terrible, Margaret.

MARGARET: So, in the inimitable words of my traveling companion, Mrs. Brynne here, what's up, doc? What's the story, Air India?

MAN: I'm afraid Business Class is completely full. So is Tourist.

MARGARET: This is outrageous. I'm going to call that travel agent.

MAN: All I have are two seats in First Class, sleeperettes.

KATHARINE: We couldn't possibly afford that.

MAN: It's a complimentary upgrade, Mrs. Brynne. It's our error. Would that be satisfactory?

KATHARINE: Satisfactory? It's fabulous. Thank you. First Class! I'm pinching myself. What's your name?

MAN: Lennie. Leonard Tuck.

KATHARINE: I'm going to write them a letter telling them how wonderful you were to us. Tuck. Leonard Tuck. Like Friar Tuck.

MAN: *Gracias.*

KATHARINE: *De nada.*

MAN: Will First Class be satisfactory, Mrs. Civil?

MARGARET: Of course it will. But I would have been perfectly happy in our own seats.

KATHARINE: What a beginning! What luck! First Class! "O for a Muse of" you know what!"

MAN: Abracadabra! (*The computer whirs. Tickets and boarding passes emerge*) See how easy that was, Mrs. Civil? (*Making another announcement*) Final call. Air India, Flight 87, direct service to Bombay. Final call, please.

MARGARET: Come on, Katharine. (*She goes*)

KATHARINE: Goodbye, America. Goodbye, husband and children. Goodbye, Greenwich, Connecticut. Goodbye, Air India terminal. Goodbye, Leonard Tuck.

MAN: Bon voyage, Mrs. Brynne.

(KATHARINE *goes. She leaves one of her flight bags behind.* MAN *closes down quickly and is gone.* GANESHA *re-appears*)

GANESHA: They're on their way. Well, almost!

(KATHARINE *rushes back on*)

KATHARINE: My flight bag! I had a flight bag.

GANESHA: She doesn't see it.

KATHARINE: Did anyone see a flight bag?

GANESHA: Or me. I have that power.

KATHARINE: Hello?

(She rushes off at the sound of the jets revving up. The sounds will grow)

GANESHA: It begins. Well, it all began long ago. World without end, amen, and all that. This particular adventure, I was meaning. These two little, insignificant, magnificent lives. (*He is shouting to be heard over the roar of the jet engines*) Can you hear me? Did you hear me? I said, these two little, insignificant, magnificent lives! I'll see you aboard at 36,000 feet. Wait for me!

(Sounds reach a deafening volume as GANESHA *hurries aboard. The stage is bare except for* KATHARINE's *flight bag.* MAN *enters. He is a* THIEF. *He picks up the flight bag and rifles through it as he exits through the audience, scattering things he doesn't want in the aisles.*

Sounds and lights reach maximum intensity, then quickly level off: the lights to the level of an airplane in the middle of the night; the sounds to the gentle, steady thrust of jet engines at cruising speed.)

Scene Two

MARGARET *and* KATHARINE *are seated in the first-class cabin. They both have headsets on.* MARGARET *is watching the movie.* KATHARINE *is listening to a cassette.*

MOVIE SOUNDTRACK: "I don't think you know what love is. Not real love. Love that enriches, love that lifts up, love that enobles. I'm talking about love in its profoundest sense. Love as everything."

CASSETTE TAPE: "All right, now that you've visualized your 10 Personal Power Goals, I want you to *choose* them. It's not I *want* to lose weight or I *want* to make a million dollars but I *choose* to meet the perfect mate, I *choose* to drive a Lexus Infinity. Ready? Take a deep breath. Hold it." (KATHARINE *inhales*)

MOVIE SOUNDTRACK: "I think you understand obsession. I think you understand control. I think you understand passion. God knows, you know how to pleasure a person with your body. There's a word for people like you—the French have one, every language does— *fatale.*"

CASSETTE TAPE: "These are vocal affirmations. I want to hear you. Don't be shy. That's right, I'm talking to *you!* All right, go. I choose–!"

KATHARINE: I choose to be happy.

MARGARET: After all that and they're still going to make love!

KATHARINE: I choose to be healthy.

MARGARET: The movies think that's the solution to everything! A lot they know!

KATHARINE: I choose to be good.

MARGARET: I'm very surprised at Air India for showing such a film. I wonder what an Indian thinks when they see–!

KATHARINE: I choose to be—!

(The plane heaves)

MARGARET: What was that?

KATHARINE: What was what?

MARGARET: The plane, it jiggled.

KATHARINE: It didn't jiggle.

MARGARET: Well it did something it shouldn't. There it goes again!

KATHARINE: It's just a little turbulence. "I choose—." Now I've forgotten what I choose. "I choose to be happy." I already said that.

MARGARET: I hate this. I hate it, I hate it.

KATHARINE: Just think of it as a bumpy road.

MARGARET: What?

KATHARINE: It will be over soon.

MARGARET: How soon?

KATHARINE: I don't know. Soon. Soon soon.

MARGARET: We should have gone TWA.

KATHARINE: TWA is for sissies. Anyone can go TWA. Air India is an adventure. I feel like we're already there.

(MAN *appears. He is a* STEWARD)

MAN: Ladies! Sshh! Please. People are sleeping.

KATHARINE: Will you tell my friend we're not going to crash?

MAN: We're not going to crash. That's the good news. The bad news is we'll be starting dinner service just as soon as we're out of this. That was a joke.

MARGARET: I'm quite aware of that. Tell me, does everyone connected with Air India think they're a comedian?

MAN: People think Indians are humorless. They think we're funny but they think we're humorless.

MARGARET: You're not funny and you're not an Indian.

MAN: On my mother's side. Her father was born in Calcutta. I was born on Teller Avenue in the Bronx. Whoa! Ride 'em cowboy! That was a good one. It's always a little dicey over this part of the Atlantic this time of the year. (*The plane heaves*) I better get back to my seat. The pilot has the Fasten Seat Belt sign on for the crew now, too. Excuse me. I shall return with your pickled herring and hot towels. The towels are tastier. (*He goes*)

KATHARINE: Does he remind you of Walter?

MARGARET: The steward? Not in the least.

KATHARINE: I didn't know you were afraid of flying.

MARGARET: I've flown over this part of the Atlantic this time of the year at least fifteen times and it was never like this.

KATHARINE: Actually, I like a little turbulence.

MARGARET: You're the type who would.

KATHARINE: It lets me know we're really up there. If it gets too quiet and still, I worry the engines have stopped and we're just going to plummet to the earth.

MARGARET: Can we talk about something else?

KATHARINE: Do you want to hold my hand?

MARGARET: Of course not.

KATHARINE: Do you want some gum?

MARGARET: Is it the kind that sticks to your crowns?

KATHARINE: I don't know.

MARGARET: If it's the kind that sticks I don't want it.

KATHARINE: You're out of luck. It must have been in the bag I left in the terminal.

MARGARET: What is it?

KATHARINE: A whistle. George made me take it. In case we get into any sort of trouble in India, I'm supposed to blow it so help will come. "Who?" I asked him. "Sabu on an elephant?"

MARGARET: Will you keep your voice down?

(The plane heaves, extra-mightily this time)

KATHARINE: This is ridiculous. Give me your hand.

MARGARET: We're all going to die.

KATHARINE: Just shut up and say a "Hail, Mary."

MARGARET: Methodists don't say "Hail, Mary."

KATHARINE: We're going to be all right.

MARGARET: Ow! That's too tight.

(The turbulence subsides)

KATHARINE: See?

MARGARET: I can bear anything as long as I know it's going to end.

KATHARINE: Remember the last year we went to St. Kitt's?

MARGARET: The men got sick from eating crayfish.

KATHARINE: They were *langoustes.*

MARGARET: They looked like crayfish.

KATHARINE: That's not the reason I never wanted to go back there.

MARGARET: Alan nearly died. Besides, it was time for a new island.

KATHARINE: It was the incident with the little plane.

MARGARET: What incident? I don't remember.

KATHARINE: Yes, you do! We were swimming in front of the hotel. A small, single-engine plane had taken off from the airport. The engine kept stalling. No one moved. It was terrifying. That little plane just floating there. No sound. No sound at all. Like a kite without a string, without a wind. I don't think I've ever felt so helpless.

MARGARET: I remember.

KATHARINE: Finally, I guess the pilot made the necessary adjustments, the engine caught and stayed caught and the little plane flew away without a worry in the world, as if nothing had happened, and we finished swimming and played tennis and after lunch you bought that Lalique vase I could still kick myself for letting you have.

MARGARET: You've envied me that piece of Lalique all these years? It's yours.

KATHARINE: I don't want it.

MARGARET: Really, I insist, Kitty. I think I only bought it because I knew you wanted it. That, and I was mad at Alan for some crack about how I looked in my new bathing suit. The plane's stopped jiggling. Smooth as glass now. Thank you.

KATHARINE: I've thought about that plane a lot. Maybe we were helpless. Maybe we weren't responsible. Maybe it wasn't our fault. But what kept that plane up there? God? A God? Some Benevolence? Prayer? Our prayers? I think everyone on that beach was praying that morning in their particular way. So maybe we aren't so helpless. Maybe we are responsible. Maybe it is our fault what happens. Maybe, maybe, maybe.

MARGARET: Do you want to give me my hand back?

KATHARINE: I'm sorry. Thank you. Did I do that? I *was* holding tight! I'm sorry. (*She kisses* MARGARET'*s hand*) What happened to your liver spots? You used to have great big liver spots.

MARGARET: Will you keep your voice down? I keep begging you to come with me. The man's a genius. And it's paradise there.

KATHARINE: And it costs 3,000 dollars a week. I'd rather go to India for my soul than some spa in Orange County for the backs of my hands.

MARGARET: Happily, you can afford both.

KATHARINE: I keep thinking about Walter.

MARGARET: Why would you do that to yourself?

KATHARINE: I can't help it.

MARGARET: Well, stop. Stop right now. Think about something else. Think about the Taj Mahal. Think about India.

KATHARINE: They say it's like a dream, the Taj Mahal.

MARGARET: I hope it's not like the Eiffel Tower. All your life you look at pictures of the Eiffel Tower and then when you actually see it, it looks just like the pictures of it. There's no resonance when you look at the Eiffel Tower. I'm expecting some resonance from the Taj Mahal. I'll be terribly disappointed if there isn't any. You're humming again, Kitty.

KATHARINE: I'm sorry.

MARGARET: You asked me to tell you.

KATHARINE: All of a sudden, I can't remember when it was built!

MARGARET: It was begun in 1632 and completed in 1654.

KATHARINE: All that reading up on it and for what!?

MARGARET: Do you remember who it was built for?

KATHARINE: Of course I do. Someone's wife.

MARGARET: Everyone knows that, Kitty. What was her name?

KATHARINE: I knew you were going to ask me that. Marilyn? Betty? Betty Mahal? I know who built it. Shah Jahan.

MARGARET: The favorite wife was Mumtaz Mahal.

KATHARINE: Mumtaz, of course! It was on the tip of my tongue.

MARGARET: It took twenty-two years and 20,000 workers to build.

KATHARINE: Is this going to be some sort of pop quiz?

MARGARET: I was trying to get your mind off Walter.

KATHARINE: Nothing will ever get my mind off Walter.

MARGARET: This is a wonderful start to a trip!

KATHARINE: I'm sorry. (*She hums a little*)

MARGARET: Kitty, sshh!, you're doing it. It's nobody's fault.

(KATHARINE *begins to read from a travel brochure she has taken out of her purse*)

KATHARINE: Now listen to this. (*She reads*) "Don't drink the water, which means absolutely no ice in your drinks or eating of washed fruit and vegetables." Sounds charming. "Above all be patient. Allow, accept, be."

MARGARET: That's what I've been telling you.

(*A light comes up on* GANESHA. *He is sitting on the wing. He wears a leather flight jacket and an aviator's white silk scarf which blows wildly in the rushing wind we can suddenly hear. He waves to* KATHARINE.)

KATHARINE (*suddenly*): What's that out there?

MARGARET: Oh, my God! Out where?

KATHARINE: Out there, on the wing!

MARGARET: I don't want to know.

KATHARINE: Margaret, look!

MARGARET: I don't want to look.

KATHARINE: There's nothing wrong. There's something wonderful out there. It's beautiful. Just look.

(MAN *appears. He is an* AGING HIPPY. *He leans over* MARGARET *to look out the window*)

MAN: What's happening? We on fire? Oh wow!

MARGARET: Do you mind!

KATHARINE: Do you see what I see?

MAN: We don't get shit like this at the back of the plane.

KATHARINE: It looks like an angel. Do you believe in angels?

MAN: Lady, I believe in everything.

MARGARET: If you'd like me to get up, so you two can continue this—.

MAN: I was just on my way to the head. You want to see some real fucking angels, pardon the expression, check out the caves in Ajanta. Angels and red monkeys. I didn't believe in shit till I checked out Ajanta.

KATHARINE: Ajanta? Is that on our itinerary, Margaret?

MARGARET: You know it is. Thank you.

MAN: Okay, okay, lady. You made your point. I'm going back to Peasant Class.

MARGARET: I didn't say a word.

MAN: You didn't have to. It was in the eyes. It's always in the eyes. You have cruel eyes. They're filled with hate. I mean that nicely. I mean that sincerely.

KATHARINE: Now just a minute.

MAN: Your friend needs a good purge in the Ganges. I don't think she's ready for Katmandu yet. There's not enough dope in the Himalayas to mellow that dude out. (*He goes*)

MARGARET: I hate it when they do that. The first class bathrooms should be for the first class passengers.

KATHARINE: Do you want me to make a citizen's arrest? Relax Margaret.

MARGARET: When did you get so serene?

KATHARINE: I took a pill.

MARGARET: I don't know why they bother to have classes if they're not going to enforce them.

KATHARINE: You don't have cruel eyes.

MARGARET: Thank you.

KATHARINE: You have beautiful eyes. Don't cry.

MARGARET: I'm not crying. Does it look like I'm crying? (*She puts her headset back on*)

KATHARINE: People like that don't know what they're saying half the time. That, or they speak before they think. Don't mind them. I've always liked your eyes.

MARGARET: I'm fine, Kitty. I'm trying to watch the movie!

(KATHARINE *watches her a moment, then puts her own headset back on.* GANESHA *shakes his head and looks up from his newspaper*)

GANESHA: Lord, Lord, Lord! Little Puck said it best: "Shiva, what fools these mortals be!" Such thoughtless, needless cruelty. Down there on earth, up here at 41,000 feet. (We went higher to avoid the turbulence while you weren't looking.) We are the ones who are powerless. We can only sigh and shake our heads. There's a serenity in being a god but very little real power. We gave it all to you.

KATHARINE: "I choose to be happy. I choose to be loving. I choose to be good."

(*She will repeat this over and over. Tears are running down* MARGARET's *cheeks as she watches the movie.* MAN *appears on the wing of the plane. He is* WALTER. *His clothes are bloodied; his features battered from the beating which killed him*)

GANESHA: Hello, Walter.

MAN: Mind if I join you out here?

GANESHA: I'd be honored.

MAN: I really have to draw the line at bad curry and movies about unrepentant heterosexuals.

GANESHA: Heterosexuals aren't so bad. Where would we be without them? Please.

(MAN *sits on the wing at* GANESHA'*s feet*)

MAN: What are you?

GANESHA: I take whatever I can get. I'm speaking about affection. Physical love was never my strong suit. I'm not that sort of god. Fag? (*He offers* MAN *a cigarette*) I'm sorry. The raj is over but the melody lingers on! The Hindi word for tobacco is *nanded.*

MAN: *Nanded,* that's a nice word. Well, nicer than "fag."

(*They will smoke*)

GANESHA: I thought that was you when we were boarding.

MAN: Where my mother goes, can this one be far behind? Listen, India has got to beat another of her annual, same old two weeks in the Caribbean with the Civils.

GANESHA: Mrs. Civil is inconsolable. You must have heard what happened.

MAN: It served her right.

GANESHA: Look at her. I hate to see a woman cry.

MAN: I don't like Mrs. Civil. Mrs. Civil didn't like me. Let her cry her stone-cold heart out. Mrs. Civil was a bitch. Is. Is a bitch. I'm the was.

GANESHA: Your words are like daggers, Walter. They cause me such pain.

MAN: Different people sing from different charts, old man.

GANESHA: Not half so old and hard as you.

KATHARINE: "I choose to be happy. I choose to be loving. I choose to be good."

GANESHA: Your mother's been thinking about you again.

MAN: I'd like her to stop. I'd like her to forget all about me.

GANESHA: There will never come that day. She loves you. You're her son.

MAN: That's not love. It's guilt that's become a curse. She should have loved me not just for falling down and scraping my knee when I was a little boy, but for standing tall when I was a young man and telling her I loved other men. She should have loved me when my heart was breaking for the love of them. She should have loved me when I wanted to tell her my heart was finally, forever full with someone —Jonathan!— but I didn't dare. She should have loved me the most when he was gone, that terrible day when my life was over.

(KATHARINE *has taken off her headset, but she will be drawn into the scene*)

KATHARINE: "I choose to be happy. I choose to be loving. I choose to be good."

MAN: Instead you waited. You waited until late one night, I was coming home, no! to our "apartment" as you always put it; "Two men can't have a 'home,' Walter"; maybe I had a little too much to drink, certainly a lot too much pain and anger to bear—

KATHARINE: I didn't know.

MAN: A car whizzes by. Voices, young voices, scream the obligatory epithets: "Fag. Queer. Cocksucker. Dead from AIDS queer meat."

GANESHA: Oh dear, oh dear!

MAN: I make the obligatory Gay '90s gesture back. (*He gives the finger*) Die from my cum, you assholes!

GANESHA: Oh dear, oh dear!

MAN: The car stops. The street is empty. Suddenly this part seems obligatory, too. Six young men pile out.

KATHARINE: Black! All of them black!

MAN: No, mother! All of them you!

MARGARET (*loudly, because of the headset*): I think we saw this movie at Watch Hill!

MAN: Six young men with chains and bats. One had a putter.

KATHARINE: Six young black men! Hoodlums! Two of them had records!

GANESHA: Oh, dear! Oh, dear! All of you!

MAN: I stood there. It seemed like it took them forever to get to where I was standing. There was a funny silence. Probably because I wasn't scared. I said "Hello." I don't know why. I hated them. I hated everything about them. I hated what they were going to do to me. I knew it would hurt. I wanted it to be quick. So I said "Hello" again. The one with the putter swung first. You could hear the sound. Woosh. Ungh! against the side of my head. I could feel the skull cracking. He'd landed a good one. Then they all started swinging and beating and kicking. I stayed on my feet a remarkably long time. I was sort of proud of me. Finally I went down and they kept on swinging and beating and kicking, only now it wasn't hurting so much. It was more abstract. I could *watch* the pain, corroborate it. Finally, they got back in their car, not speaking anymore. They weren't having such a good time either anymore, I guess. None of us were. I was just lying there, couldn't move, couldn't speak, when I could hear their car screeching a U-turn and it coming towards me, real fast, just swerving at the last minute, only missing my head by about this much. What I figure is this: they

were gonna run me over, but at the last second one of them
grabbed the wheel. So they weren't one hundred percent animal.
One of them had a little humanity. Just a touch. Maybe. If my
theory's right, that is. But that's when you waited to love me,
mama.

KATHARINE: I always loved you.

MAN: That's when you waited to know it.

KATHARINE: Why are you doing this?

MAN: Let me go. Let us both go.

KATHARINE: I can't. You're my firstborn.

MAN: There's Pop. There's Jerry. There's sis and the kids.

KATHARINE: You were my favorite.

MAN: You were mine. We killed each other.

KATHARINE: Where's your scarf? You'll catch a chill without your scarf.

MAN: You sound like Jonathan.

KATHARINE: Give me a kiss.

MAN: No, I don't want to kiss you.

KATHARINE: You will. (*She puts her headset back on*)

MAN: Pop! I never called dad "Pop" in my entire life! It must be the
altitude.

(*He goes.* MARGARET *takes off her headset in disgust with the movie. She
has stopped crying*)

MARGARET: And they all lived happily ever after. Sure they did. (*She sees that* KATHARINE *is crying now. She takes her hand soothingly*) It's all right. It's all right.

KATHARINE: "I choose to be happy. I choose to be loving. I choose to be good."

(Lights begin to fade on the two women)

GANESHA: Oh dear, oh dear! Let's go to India! (*He claps his hands twice. Music. The sound of the jet engines will fade away and all we will hear are the delicate sounds of a wooden flute.* GANESHA *has pulled down a map of the subcontinent*) India, a republic in South Asia; comprises most of former British India and the semi-independent Indian States and Agencies; became a dominion in 1947; became fully independent on January 26, 1950, with membership in the British Commonwealth of Nations. Population as of the last census: 813 million. Area: 1,246,880 square miles. Principal language: Hindi. I was born right here. Kerola. The most beautiful part of India. The beaches alone. The temples at Tiruchirappalli (trust me, but don't ask me to spell it). How I was born is a very interesting story. Some say I was created out of a mother's loneliness. Some say I was the expression of a woman's deepest need. I say: I don't know. What child does?

Scene Three

MAN *appears. He is a* PORTER *at the Bombay airport. He has* KATHARINE *and* MARGARET'*s luggage on a dolly.*

KATHARINE: Wait! Stop! Stop right there! Come back with those.

GANESHA: Excuse me. They've landed and things are getting quite out of hand at the Bombay airport.

KATHARINE: I had eight pieces. Something is missing. One, two, three . . . !

MARGARET: Where's the guide? They said he'd be waiting with a sign with our names on it.

KATHARINE: There's only seven now. I know I had eight.

MARGARET: When we got off the plane, they said he'll meet you at customs. At customs, they said he'll meet you just outside customs. Now we're outside customs and there's not even someone to tell us the next place he's not going to meet us!

KATHARINE: I know what's missing: my cassette player with all my tapes. All my Frank Sinatra and Mozart and Cole Porter. This is terrible. Do you speak English, young man? Do you understand? He doesn't speak English.

GANESHA (*stepping forward to greet them, wearing a blazer*): Mrs. Alan Civil? Mrs. George Brynne?

MARGARET: Thank God!

GANESHA: You're welcome, Mrs. Civil. Just a little joke.

KATHARINE: And you are?

GANESHA: Your representative from Red Carpet Tours. I have a car and driver waiting for you at the curb. Your suite at the Taj Palace is in order. You have a most excellent view of the harbor and the Gate of India. Come.

KATHARINE: I'm missing something. A cassette player and all my tapes.

GANESHA: Did you take her cassette player?

MAN: What do you think?

GANESHA: I think you should give it back to her.

MAN: Get lost, pop.

GANESHA: Is this the impression you want our country to make?

MAN: Well it's a little more honest than yours. "You have a most excellent view of the harbor and Gate of India." I'll show the ladies a most excellent view of my ass.

KATHARINE: What are they saying?

MARGARET: I don't speak Hindi, Kitty.

KATHARINE: Why are you snapping at me?

MARGARET: I've been up for a day and a half on a plane. I'd like to get to our hotel.

KATHARINE: So would I.

MARGARET: I don't know why this should call for a big discussion. What's he saying?

GANESHA: He says he will check the lost and found and bring your player to the hotel if it is returned.

KATHARINE: Returned? That means someone took it!

GANESHA: I meant "found." I translated badly.

(MAN *starts wheeling the luggage off on his dolly*)

KATHARINE: Where's he going?

GANESHA: Not to worry. I told him to start loading the boot.

KATHARINE: That's it for the cassette player? Don't I get a receipt, a claim check or something?

GANESHA: Leave everything to me.

MARGARET: What do you want him to do, Katharine? Mrs. Brynne is a loser. I mean she loses things. That came out badly in translation, too.

GANESHA: Come. A soft bed and India await you.

KATHARINE: Just a minute. I want to take all this in.

MARGARET: What is there to take in, Kitty? It's an airport. (KATHARINE *doesn't budge.* MARGARET *sighs audibly*) Hurry up if you're going to do that. (*To* GANESHA) Mrs. Brynne is also something of an enthusiast.

(MARGARET *and* GANESHA *start walking off.* KATHARINE *will remain*)

GANESHA: What would you like to know about Bombay?

MARGARET: Nearly everything but not right now. I'm too tired.

GANESHA: It's very big, Bombay.

MARGARET: So was China.

(*They are gone*)

KATHARINE: "O for a muse of fire"! I'm not going to let a missing
cassette player spoil this. The world is filled with ill-manufactured
cassette players from Taiwan but only one me, Katharine Brynne,
née Mitchell, born too many years ago in a ridiculous place when I
consider to where I've come, experiencing this one particular and
special moment. Look. Attack things with your eyes. See them
fiercely. Listen. Hear everything, ignore nothing. Smell. Breathe
deeper than you've ever dared. Experience. Be. But above all, remember. Carve adamantine letters in your brain: "This I have seen
and done and known." Amen. No, above all, *feel!* Take my heart
and do with it what you will. (*She takes a long look at the terminal*)
Yes.

(*Lights change to make transition to next scene but* KATHARINE *stays
where she is. Music.* GANESHA *appears*)

GANESHA: There are three people you must know about in my story.
(*He pulls down a chart with the appropriate pictures*) My mother,
Parvati (isn't she lovely?), my father, Shiva and me. One day, before
I was born, my mother, Parvati, was sitting in her bath. She told an
attendant to let no one enter, not even Shiva, her lord and master.
But Shiva is everyone's lord and master and no one dared bar him
from entering his wife's bath. Parvati covered herself in shame, she
had no prestige now, but she was angry, too. Some say she decided
then and there she must have a gana of her own. A gana is someone
obedient to our will and our will alone. No woman had ever had a
gana of her own. This is what happened: my mother Parvati gath-
ered the saffron paste from her own body and with her own hand
created a boy, her first born, her gana, me! Oh how lovely it is to be
born! We were so happy!

(*Lights have changed. We are in a hotel room.*)

Scene Four

A hotel room with an overhead fan and a balcony. MARGARET is reading from a guide book. KATHARINE is listening to GANESHA.

MARGARET: I'm a little worried how we're going to handle your poverty, Mr. Vitankar.

KATHARINE: Maggie, please, we're right in the middle of something important.

MARGARET: I thought he was finished.

KATHARINE: I'm sorry, Mr. Vitankar.

GANESHA: It's quite all right. I'm sure you'll be handling it very well indeed, Mrs. Civil. Your poverty is angry. Ours is not. In India, poverty is not an emotion. It's a fact.

MARGARET: What about the status of women in India?

GANESHA: The lot of women in India is very, very dismal. We set you on fire when you don't obey and expect you to set yourselves on fire to show proper mourning when we die. Does that answer your question?

MARGARET: I think so.

KATHARINE: That's dreadful.

GANESHA: But we're a democracy now. That's the main thing to know about us. The largest democracy in the world. So maybe there's hope for you ladies yet. Change things. Vote. Tell us men where to go. You're very tired. We'll continue the story of Lord Ganesh tomorrow.

KATHARINE: You have so many gods! Keeping them straight! Vishnu, Parvati, Ganesh! He sounds like a Jewish food.

GANESHA: No offense, but Lord Ganesha is better than a bagel.

KATHARINE: We're not offended. We're not Jewish.

GANESHA: Tomorrow morning then? Eight o'clock. (MAN *is now a* WAITER. *He carries a tray with two Coca Colas*) The ladies asked for Diet Pepsi.

MARGARET: That's all right.

MAN: The ladies are fortunate to get anything at this hour.

GANESHA: You are a very rude waiter, young man.

MAN: We're a union now. I don't have to be polite to anyone.

GANESHA: He said the hotel is out of Diet Pepsi and a million apologies.

MARGARET: It's a wonderful language. It almost sounds like Japanese.

MAN: What is she saying?

GANESHA: She agrees. You're a very rude waiter, young man. Shame on you.

MAN: Shame on me? Shame on you. These are Jew Christian old whores with white saggy skin. Their shit is on your tongue from all the ass licking. You are no Indian. You are no one. Tell them in your perfect English that I'm waiting for my tip. For another 20 rupees I will fuck them.

MARGARET: See what I mean, Kitty? It's more the rhythm than the sound of Japanese.

(GANESHA *gives* MAN *a tip*)

MAN: Thank you, papa India. Thank you, *babu*. I smile at the ladies. I exit the room backwards and bowing. I wish the old bags a good night.

(He smiles and is gone)

MARGARET: Thank you.

KATHARINE: *Muchas gracias!*

MARGARET: That smile! Those wonderful teeth against that wonderful dark skin! It's like ebony. No, mahogany! Are all Indian men such heartbreakers, Mr. . . . I'm sorry.

GANESHA: Mr. Vitanker.

(The telephone rings)

KATHARINE *(answering phone)*: Hello? Hello?

MARGARET: Till tomorrow then, Mr. Vitankar. Good night.

GANESHA *(taking his leave)*: Mrs. Civil, Mrs. Brynne.

KATHARINE *(still into phone)*: Hello? *(To* GANESHA*)* Goodbye! *Gracias! Muchas gracias!*

GANESHA: *De nada.*

KATHARINE *(back into phone)*: Hello? There's no one there.

GANESHA: Now you're truly in India.

(He bows, backs himself out of the room, much as the MAN/PORTER *did)*

MARGARET: Really, Katharine!

KATHARINE: What?

MARGARET: That is so patronizing!

KATHARINE: What is?

MARGARET: Speaking Spanish to an Indian. What is that? Your generic Third World "thank you"?

KATHARINE: I'm sorry, but I don't know the word for "thank you" in Hindi.

MARGARET: Well, it isn't *gracias!*

KATHARINE: He knew what I meant.

MARGARET: He would have known what you meant in your native language. *Gracias* reduces him to the level of a peon and you to that of a horrid tourist.

KATHARINE: My intention was to thank him, Margaret. On that level I think my *gracias* was highly effective. Now which bed would you like?

MARGARET: It's really of no interest to me.

KATHARINE: I wish you would adopt such a generous attitude towards me. I'll take this one then. I hope you remembered the alarm clock. That was your responsibility!

(They have begun to unpack)

MARGARET: I'm sorry, but if we're going to travel together you've got to understand something about me. I am very sensitive to the feelings of others.

KATHARINE: You could have fooled me.

MARGARET: Frankly, you've said and done several things that have offended me since we got on the plane. No, "offended" is too strong a word. Let's say "embarrassed." There! I've said it and I'm glad. The air is cleared.

KATHARINE: Don't stop now, Margaret, I'm all ears.

MARGARET: You're sure?

KATHARINE: Absolutely! If we're going to "travel together" for the next two weeks, let's have absolute candor. I hate that outfit.

MARGARET: Be serious! That remark about Jewish food just now. I could have died. Comparing one of their gods to a bagel.

KATHARINE: He compared him to a bagel. I only said he sounded like something Jewish you ate.

MARGARET: Will you keep your voice down?

KATHARINE: No! And stop saying that. I am sick and tired of being told to keep my voice down when I am not in the wrong. And even if I were in the wrong, you have no business telling me to keep my voice down. I am not your cowed daughter or your catatonic husband and I am not about to become your cowed and catatonic traveling companion. I'm me. You're you. Respect the difference or go home. I came to India to have an adventure. This is not an adventure. This is the same old Shinola.

MARGARET: Well it's nice to know what your best friend really thinks of you. And your family.

KATHARINE: I didn't mean that. I'm very fond of Joy. And Alan's just quiet around us. I'm sure he's quite talkative when you two are alone.

MARGARET: Not especially.

KATHARINE: I'll give you "O for a muse of fire." I probably do it just to annoy you, like you and the Lalique.

MARGARET: Every time you say it, I say to myself "O for someone who didn't say 'O for a muse of fire' at the drop of a hat."

KATHARINE: It wouldn't bother me if you did.

MARGARET: Well that's the difference between us.

KATHARINE: If you can't respect it, at least observe it.

MARGARET: You've changed. Ever since you went to those lectures in Bridgeport, Nurturing your Inner Child! You know what I say? Stifle him! If we all nurtured our inner child, Katharine, this planet would come to a grinding halt while we all had a good cry.

KATHARINE: Well maybe it should.

(There is a pause. They are each lost in their own particular thoughts. When they take a breath and sigh, it will be together)

MARGARET: "O for a muse of fire" is right! Bartender! One fiery muse, a decent analyst and an extra-dry gin martini.

KATHARINE: Don't say that. I think it's wonderful what you've done. I couldn't have done it.

MARGARET: I finally know what the skin of your teeth means. It's a layer you don't want to be involved with. Anyway, I'm sorry I let it get under my skin. Not you, "it."

KATHARINE: It's Shakespeare. "Muse of fire."

MARGARET: I know that. That is so patronizing to tell me it's Shakespeare!

KATHARINE: I didn't know it until they showed it on Public Television. It's the first line of "Henry V." How hard it is to really describe anything. And I have that trouble, don't you?

MARGARET: I don't know. Probably.

KATHARINE: "Muse of Fire" is my talisman. It's my way of telling myself "Savor this moment, Katharine Brynne *née* Mitchell. Relish it.
It is important. You'll never be here or feel this way again."

MARGARET: This is what I mean. Those lectures in Bridgeport.

KATHARINE: That's not nurturing my Inner Child. It's Shakespeare.
Telling you you can be a pain in the ass is nurturing my Inner
Child.

MARGARET: Now I'm a pain in the ass!

*(They have finished unpacking and will now begin to make ready for
bed)*

KATHARINE: I didn't say you were a pain in the ass. I said you could be
a pain in the ass. I'm hoping the next two weeks you won't be.

(The phone begins to ring. This time MARGARET *will answer it)*

MARGARET: I have never been a pain in the ass for two entire weeks.
Have I? *(Into phone)* Hello?

KATHARINE: That's right, we were only in Barbados for eleven days.

MARGARET: Blame that trip on Barbados, not me! Hello?

KATHARINE: Everyone's toilet was broken.

MARGARET: Seven years later she throws Barbados in my face! Hello?
(She hangs up) There's no one there.

KATHARINE: I hope you haven't come to India for their telephones *or*
the plumbing!

MARGARET: There you go again! Patronizing! I've come to India for
personal reasons. Just as you've come for yours.

KATHARINE: I thought we came to India for a vacation.

Dominic Cuskern as Ganesha.

All photos of the 1993 Manhattan Theatre Club production by Gerry Goodstein.

Zoe Caldwell (left) as Katharine with Frances Sternhagen as Margaret.

Frances Sternhagen (left) with Zoe Caldwell.

(From left to right) Zoe Caldwell, Dominic Cuskern, Fisher Stevens (as Man) and Frances Sternhagen.

MARGARET: I adore you, Kitty, even when you're impossible.

KATHARINE: No, you don't. I don't think we are best friends. I don't think we know each other at all.

MARGARET: I'm sorry you feel that way. I feel very warmly towards you.

KATHARINE: I know. Me, too.

MARGARET: It's going to be fine. From this moment on, we're going to get along famously and become the very best of friends.

KATHARINE: Who says?

MARGARET: My Inner Child. Do you mind if I nip in the loo first?

KATHARINE: Where do you think we are, luv, the Dorchester? (MARGA-RET *goes into the bathroom area of their hotel room*) We have a balcony. Did you know we had a balcony? We have two of them! (*She steps forward onto the balcony*)

MARGARET: How does the rest of it go? Do you know? "O for a muse of fire" *what?*

(KATHARINE *stands looking at the harbor in front of the hotel. She is overwhelmed by what she sees*)

KATHARINE: "O for a Muse of fire, that would ascend
    The brightest heaven of invention!"

(MARGARET *screams in the bathroom*)

MARGARET: Don't mind me. It's only a waterbug the size of a standard poodle.

KATHARINE: "A kingdom for a stage, princes to act,
    And monarchs to behold the swelling scene!"
    Well something like that.

(The MAN *has appeared on an adjoining balcony. He is* HARRY, *a young man)*

MAN: Very good.

KATHARINE: Hello.

MAN: Hi. Fairly spectacular, isn't it? Especially this time of almost-morning, not-quite-dawn. We couldn't sleep.

KATHARINE: We just got in.

MAN: "Then should the warlike Harry, like himself,
Assume the port of Mars; and at his heels,
Leashed in like hounds, should famine, sword, and fire
Crouch for employment."

KATHARINE: Very good yourself!

MAN: I have no idea what it means: "Crouch for employment"?

KATHARINE: I like the sound of it!

MAN: And I did that part! I wore red tights and everyone said I had terrific legs. No one mentioned my performance.

KATHARINE: You're an actor?

MAN: For one brief shining hour in college. I'm a doctor. Or I was. I'm sick now. A physician who cannot heal himself.

KATHARINE: I'm sorry.

MAN: "But pardon, gentles all,
The flat unraised spirits that hath dared
On this unworthy scaffold to bring forth
So great an object." Deedle-diddle-dee.
You've got to help me here.

KATHARINE: "Can this cockpit hold
The vasty fields of France? Or may we cram
Within this wooden O". . . .
That's my favorite part.

MAN: Me, too. "This wooden O"!

KATHARINE: "Within this wooden O the very casques"—

MAN (*very loud and heroic*): "That did affright the air at Agincourt?"
(*his last words ring in the night air*)

MARGARET: Kitty? What's going on out there?

MAN (*over his shoulder*): Okay, we'll keep it down, Ben. Sorry. (*To*
KATHARINE) He's got his hands full with this one.

KATHARINE: So does Mrs. Civil.

MAN: You're traveling with someone you call Mrs. Civil? This is very
Tennessee Williams or very Dickensian, I can't decide which.

KATHARINE: Well I don't call her Mrs. Civil. Her name is Margaret. I'm
Katharine, Kate, Kitty, I've been called everything. I prefer Katharine.

MAN: Hello, Katharine. I'm Harry.

KATHARINE: Katharine Brynne.

MAN: Harold Walter Strong.

KATHARINE: I had a son named Walter.

MAN: I'm sorry.

KATHARINE: Me, too.

MAN: How long has it been?

KATHARINE: Three years, feels like yesterday. Is that the Gate of India?

MAN: It was built for Queen Victoria's Jubilee Visit to her prize colony. She never came. I guess she had something better to do. The British have a real attitude problem when it comes to anyone else, especially wogs. (Their not-so-nice word for people of a certain color.) God knows, they loathe us. (I'm assuming you're a Yank.) All that "luv" and "darling" and "Ta ta, duckie" and they hate our guts. Ask me how I know all this? Did I spend a term at Oxford? No. Did I rent rooms for the season in Belgravia? No. I'm talking off the top of my head. It's just a feeling I have. I'll shut up and watch the sun rise over Bombay Harbor with you. (*By now we should be aware that* KATHARINE *is humming again*) What's that you're humming?

KATHARINE: Oh, nothing, I'm sorry.

MAN: "Blow The Wind Southerly," right?

KATHARINE: I don't know.

MAN: It is. I love that song. (*He begins to sing*)

KATHARINE: Please. Don't. I couldn't bear it. It was my son's favorite song.

MAN: I understand. I'll tell him he had good taste in music and mothers.

KATHARINE: Don't talk like that.

(GANESHA *comes out on the terrace with* MAN)

GANESHA: You're barefoot. Where are your slippers? And your robe! You're drenched. Jesus! You're soaking wet.

MAN: This is Ben, Katharine. He worries about me. That's all right, I worry about him. We're neither of us terribly well.

GANESHA: Hello, Katharine. Excuse me. You're burning up.

MAN: I'm freezing actually!

(MARGARET *comes out of the bathroom area of their room. She is brushing her teeth*)

MARGARET: It's all yours, Kitty!

(*She will go out onto another balcony off their hotel room*)

GANESHA: I'll get your robe.

MAN: I can do it.

(*They exit,* GANESHA *supporting* MAN)

MARGARET: I said it's all yours. I picked up Crest gel instead of their toothpaste. I'm always doing that. I think they make the boxes almost identical just to confuse people. Why do they do that? I hate gel. It sticks to my fingers. I guess that's the Gate of India, Bombay Harbor and the Indian Ocean beyond. I guess we're here. We're really, really here. What is all that down there, Kitty? In the square, the plaza, in front of the hotel and all around the Gate? It's like something moving.

KATHARINE: It's people sleeping.

MARGARET: It's too dense for people.

KATHARINE: It's people.

MARGARET: Then it's all people. There's no place we're seeing the pavement then. Wall to wall people.

KATHARINE: I think it's beautiful.

MARGARET: I'm sure they don't. Excuse me, I've got to spit again.

(She goes back to bathroom area)

KATHARINE *(singing, softly, to herself)*:
"Blow the wind southerly, southerly, southerly
Blow the wind south o'er the bonny blue sea.
Blow the wind southerly, southerly, southerly
Blow bonny breeze my lover to me.

(She has trouble continuing. GANESHA *has appeared on an adjoining balcony)*

They told me last night there were ships in the offing
And I hurried down to the deep rolling sea.
But my eye could not see it, wherever might be it
The bark that is bearing my lover to me."

GANESHA: Don't stop.

KATHARINE: I'm sorry. I should have realized. Everyone's doors are open.

GANESHA: My wife said, "Listen, Toshiro. Listen, an angel is singing."

KATHARINE: I'm hardly an angel, I have the voice of a frog and truly, I didn't mean to wake you.

GANESHA: Why are you crying, Mrs. Brynne?

KATHARINE: I'm not crying.

GANESHA: May I assuage your tears?

KATHARINE: I said, I'm not crying.

GANESHA: I would like to help you.

KATHARINE: How do you know my name?

GANESHA: We were going through customs. I see I made very little impression. Permit me to introduce myself again. Toshiro Wattanabe of Nagasaki. My wife is Yuriko.

KATHARINE: If you say so.

GANESHA: Be careful of India, Mrs. Brynne. Be very careful here. If you're not, you may find yourself here.

KATHARINE: You sound like someone in a very bad novel or movie or play about India.

GANESHA: Lord knows we've had our fill of them!

KATHARINE: I came to India because I didn't want to go to some mindless resort in the Caribbean with our two husbands for the ninetieth year in a row and the children and the in–laws and the cats and the dogs and the turtles are all out of the house or dead or married and no one is especially depending on me right now. This is my turn.

GANESHA: Why India?

KATHARINE: Why not?

GANESHA: Why not the Grand Canyon? Why not Niagara Falls? Why not Disneyland? Why India?

KATHARINE: I heard it could heal. And now I sound like someone in a very bad novel or movie.

GANESHA: What part of you needs healing, Mrs. Brynne?

KATHARINE: I thought you Japanese were very circumspect. You go right for the jugular, Mr. . . .

GANESHA: Wattanabe. I am one singular Nipponese, Mrs. Brynne!

(MAN *is heard off calling to* GANESHA)

MAN: Toshiro!

GANESHA (over his shoulder): I'm coming, Buttercup, I'm coming! (to
KATHARINE) You think it is only your heart that is broken. May I be
so bold as to suggest it is your soul that is crying out in this Indian
dawn. Hearts can be mended. Time can heal them. But
souls . . . ! Tricky, tricky business, souls. I wish you well. You've
come to the right place. Ciao, Mrs. Brynne, sayonara.

(He goes. MARGARET returns. She is in a nightgown. She goes to "her"
adjoining balcony)

MARGARET: Sorry I took so long. I . . .

KATHARINE: What?

MARGARET: Never mind. It's all yours for good now.

KATHARINE: This view is extraordinary. See? They are people. Thousands and thousands and thousands of people.

MARGARET: More like hundreds, Kitty. Dreadful! Well, don't say they
didn't warn us. We were warned!

KATHARINE: Extraordinary!

MARGARET: I thought I heard voices out here. Were you talking to
someone?

KATHARINE: Our neighbor, one very outspoken Jap.

MARGARET: Oh my God, I hope you didn't call him that, Kitty! To his
face!

KATHARINE: I don't remember.

MARGARET: They're not Japs, you don't call them Japs anymore, the war
is over! They're Japanese. You're going to start an international
incident.

KATHARINE: I think I called him an Oriental.

MARGARET: That's just as bad. It's worse. Oriental conjures up flying carpets, Sheherazade and chop suey.

KATHARINE: Whatever I called him, he didn't seem to mind.

MARGARET: Then he was being polite. Everyone minds being called something.

KATHARINE: Can we just enjoy this?

MARGARET: We should be sleeping.

KATHARINE: I'm too excited to sleep. Let's go down there.

MARGARET: What? Are you mad? Do you know what time it is?

KATHARINE: I just want to walk among them. Experience them.

MARGARET: You can experience them from up here.

KATHARINE: Don't you feel drawn to be a part of all that?

MARGARET: No.

KATHARINE: Come with me. Before it gets light. They won't know we're tourists.

MARGARET: I'm not dressed.

KATHARINE: I'm scared to do it alone.

MARGARET: I'd be scared to do it with an army. You can't just throw yourself into a mob of homeless, dirty, disease-ridden beggars your first hour here, Kitty.

KATHARINE: Who says?

MARGARET: What if there are lepers down there?

KATHARINE: I hope there are. Yes or no?

MARGARET: No.

KATHARINE: I'll wave up at you. (*She goes*)

MARGARET: Katharine! (*Almost at once the phone begins to ring*) Hello? Hello?

(*She hangs the phone up. She goes back onto the balcony.* GANESHA *has come back onto an adjoining balcony. He is wearing a colorful silk kimono*)

GANESHA: My husband said you were upset. May I be of help?

MARGARET: Your husband was talking to my traveling companion, Mrs. Brynne.

GANESHA: Ah! And you? What about you?

MARGARET: I'm fine. No, I'm not. That's a beautiful wrap.

GANESHA: What's wrong?

MARGARET: I'm not very good at keeping an eye on people. They rush out into danger and I'm helpless to save them. I've just lost Mrs. Brynne in that still sleeping, just stirring crowd down there.

GANESHA: Your friend is in no physical danger.

MARGARET: Is there any other kind?

GANESHA: Yes. I heard you cry out in the bathroom. I'm sorry, but the air vents, I couldn't help but hear.

MARGARET: Oh, that! An enormous insect. I'm terrified of bugs. I'm sure the entire hotel heard me.

GANESHA: Twice you cried out. The second time was very soft. "Oh!", you went, just "oh!"

MARGARET: There's a lump in my breast. I keep hoping it will go away. From time to time I touch it and it's always larger.

GANESHA: May I?

(MARGARET *allows* GANESHA *to touch her*)

MARGARET: My first night in India and I'm allowing a strange woman in a gorgeous silk kimono that I covet —it's the other one— to touch my right breast. There you are. Home base. Feel it?

GANESHA: Oh!

MARGARET: You don't have to say anything.

GANESHA: Does your friend know?

MARGARET: She has enough troubles. We both do.

GANESHA: You're such a sad woman, Mrs. Civil. I'm so sorry.

MARGARET: Everyone thinks I'm a bossy bitch.

GANESHA: It's a clever defense.

MARGARET: I even fool Alan. Kitty's the one everyone loves. People like Kitty just have to be born to be loved. I've always had to work at it. I had my big chance and blew it. A son, my firstborn. His name was Gabriel. Such a beautiful name. Such a beautiful child. Gabriel. Never Gabe. Alan chose it. I used to love just saying it. Gabriel. Gabriel.

GANESHA: What happened?

MARGARET: I don't want to tell you. Where's Kitty? I don't see Kitty. We were in a park. Abingdon Square, Greenwich Village, in New York City. You wouldn't know it.

GANESHA: Where Bleecker and Hudson and Eighth Avenue all converge, just above Bank Street. Go on.

MARGARET: I'd just bought him a Good Humor bar. Maybe you know them, too?

GANESHA: Oh, yes; oh, yes! They're "sclumptious"!

MARGARET: His little face was covered with chocolate. I took a handkerchief out of my purse and wetted it with my tongue to clean his face. He pulled away from me. "No!" I pulled him back. "Yes!" Our eyes met. He looked at me with such hate . . . no! anger! . . . and pulled away again, this time hurting me. I rose to chase him but he was off the curb and into the street and under the wheels of a car before I could save him. Isn't that what mothers are supposed to do? Save their children. His head was crushed. He was dead when I picked him up. I knew. I wouldn't let anyone else hold him. They say I carried him all the way to the hospital a few blocks away. I don't remember.

GANESHA: St. Vincent's. It's very famous. Dylan Thomas and Billie Holiday died there. I'm sorry.

MARGARET: He was four years old. Gorgeous blond curls I kept long— you could then. I think he would have grown up to be a prince among men.

GANESHA: All mothers do.

MARGARET: Do you have children?

GANESHA: No, and sometimes it is a great sadness to me. But only sometimes.

MARGARET: I don't know why I told you this. Strangers in the night. Scooby-dooby-do.

GANESHA: No, new friends in the Indian dawn.

MARGARET: I've never told anyone about Gabriel. His brother and sister who came after. What would be the point? Alan and I never talk about it. This was years and years and years ago. We moved, we started a new family. I have another life. I wish I saw Kitty down there. The woman who drove the car was a black woman. We called them Negroes then. It wasn't her fault. She was devastated. I felt so sorry for her. During the service, Episcopalian, Alan's side of the family insisted, we're simple Methodist, we all heard a strange sound. Very faint at first. (GANESHA *has begun to hum the spiritual,* "Swing Low, Sweet Chariot") We weren't sure what we were hearing or if we were hearing anything at all. I thought it was the organ but we hadn't asked for one. It was the Negro woman whose car had struck my son. She'd come to the funeral. I don't know how she heard about it. She was sitting by herself in a pew at the back. She was just humming but the sound was so rich, so full, no wonder I'd thought it was the organ. The minister tried to continue but eventually he stopped and we all just turned and listened to her. Her eyes were closed. Tears were streaming down her cheeks. Such a vibrant, comforting sound it was! Her voice rose, higher and higher, loud now, magnificent, like a bright shining sword. And then the words came. (*She sings in a voice not at all like the one she has just described*)
"Swing low, sweet chariot,
Comin' for to carry me home.
Swing low, sweet chariot,
Comin' for to carry me home.

(GANESHA *joins her*)

"Swing low, sweet chariot,
Comin' for to carry me home.
Swing low, sweet chariot,
Comin' for to carry me home."

GANESHA: You're shivering. Here. Put this on. Lovely! It's yours. (*He puts the kimono over her shoulders*)

MARGARET: I couldn't.

GANESHA: Please, I insist.

MARGARET: It's not warranted, such kindness. (*Lights come up on* KATHA-RINE *and* MAN *in a different part of the stage. They are "walking" down on the street as they talk. A turntable would be useful to accomplish this effect of walking and talking*) There she is!

KATHARINE: This is wonderful. Even more wonderful than I'd imagined. Sshh! We don't want to wake them. The light will do that soon enough. We have all this just to ourselves for a little while longer and then we'll disappear into it. Are you scared?

MAN: No. Am I nervous? Yes. Am I ready to run like hell back up to my room and Ben? You bet. Careful!

KATHARINE: I thought it was a—.

MAN: It's a person.

KATHARINE: We must hold hands and we must never let go of each other.

MAN: It's a deal. Are you always so adventurous?

KATHARINE: Almost never. It's India.

GANESHA: That young man is going to die soon. So is his gentleman friend.

MARGARET: Must they?

GANESHA: Yes.

KATHARINE: Is this too fast for you?

MAN: Well, maybe a tad, Mrs. Brynne.

KATHARINE: You must call me Katharine and we shall be great friends forever and ever.

MAN: It's going to be a scorcher.

KATHARINE: Have you done Elephanta Island yet?

MAN: Our first day. Frankly, I was disappointed. They're Buddhist. I came to India for the Hindu stuff. Ben adored them. Of course, I fell, which didn't exactly help the festivities. Be careful getting off the ferry.

KATHARINE: Thank you. We will.

MARGARET (*to* GANESHA): Why must they die?

GANESHA (*with the slightest of shrugs*): Why not?

MAN: I'm afraid my Ben is going to be rather annoyed with you when he finds out I joined you down here in the madding crowd. He prefers to stay far from it. I've been dying to do this all week. (*He looks up and sees* MARGARET *and* GANESHA *on the balconies looking down at them*) Look up there! We're being watched. (*He calls up to* GANESHA) Good morning! Thank your husband for the cough syrup. It was very helpful.

KATHARINE: She can't hear you.

MARGARET: Kitty! Up here!

GANESHA: She can't hear you. Excuse me. I'm wanted elsewhere.

MARGARET: I can't accept this. You must let me give you something.

GANESHA: There's no need.

MARGARET: Do you smoke? I brought scads of cigarettes.

GANESHA: *Sayonara,* Mrs. Civil.

MARGARET: Goodbye.

(He goes. MARGARET *remains on balcony.*

During the following, although the stage is almost bare, we will hear the sounds of many, many people. Dogs barking. Vendors. Intense crowds. India.

KATHARINE *and* MAN *have re-appeared on the street below* MARGARET's *balcony)*

KATHARINE: I don't believe it, Harry! Almost the first thing I see in India and it's a cliché. I asked for a Muse of Fire and I get a bloody snake charmer!

MAN: Since when is a man in rags squatting on the pavement playing a wooden flute making a cobra coil out of a straw basket such a cliché for a lady from Connecticut? Can we stop a minute?

KATHARINE: I'm sorry. People probably think I'm your mother.

MAN: I'm sure my own mother wishes you were.

KATHARINE: What do you mean?

MAN: We don't get on. Let's keep walking. They're starting to wake up. You'll be getting the good ol' rope trick next!

KATHARINE: It serves me right. Thinking I would find India, experience it, my first morning here. But you see, Harry, I have a dream of this place, a dream of India.

MAN: I think we all do who come here, Katharine. Mine's easy. I want Ben and I to get well. If there's a choice, me first. I'm petty.

KATHARINE: No, you're not. My dream of India is this: that I am engulfed by it. That I am lost in a vast crowd such as this and become a part of it. That I'm devoured by it somehow, Harry.

MAN: I understand.

KATHARINE: It's a terrifying dream but I have to walk through it. It's a dream of death, but purgation and renewal, too. (*A light has come up on* GANESHA *sitting on the ground in a beggar's attitude. As* KATHARINE *moves towards him, the* MAN *will recede as she leaves him behind*) Look! (GANESHA *takes off his elephant's head. It is the first time we have seen his face. He is a leper. He is hideous*) When I was a very young woman I wrote something in my diary that I've never wanted anyone to know until now. This was before George. Before Walter. Before any of them. This is what I wrote, Harry. (HARRY *is gone by now*) "Before I die, I want to kiss a leper fully on the mouth and not feel revulsion. I want to cradle an oozing, ulcerous fellow human against my breast and feel love. Katharine Mitchell." (GANESHA *has opened his arms to her, half-begging, half-inviting her to come to him*) That's why I've come to India. I don't think I can do it, Harry. (*She turns to him for support. He isn't there*) Harry? Harry?

MARGARET (*waving wildly*): Kitty, come up now! It's getting light!

KATHARINE: Harry, where are you? O God, if he's fallen somewhere in this crowd. Harry!

(*The sounds of India are getting louder and louder. It is the roar of a vast multitude, the tumult of humanity. It is more like a vibration than a sound. Ideally, we will all* feel *it as well as hear it*)

MARGARET: Kitty! Look up here! I'm calling you!

KATHARINE: Harry! Please! Don't do this! Where are you! Margaret!

MARGARET: She can't hear me. Something's wrong. Just come up now! (KATHARINE *begins to blow on the whistle* GEORGE *gave her*) Kitty! Kitty! Kitty!

KATHARINE: Please, someone, help!

MARGARET: I can't hear you . . . Kitty, Kitty . . .

KATHARINE: I've lost someone, a young man, he's not well, he may have
fallen.

(She blows and blows the whistle, as MARGARET *continues to call down
from the balcony.*

The roaring is almost unendurable.

GANESHA *claps his hands together. Once and all sounds stop. Twice and
the others all freeze. The third time and all the lights snap off for the
end of Act One.)*

ACT TWO

ACT II
Scene One

Another hotel room. The telephone is heard ringing wanly. We can also hear the sound of MARGARET *being sick in the bathroom off.* GANESHA *is working a carpet sweeper over a patch of very old, very thin rug. As he works, he watches a Hindi soap opera on the television set. The* MAN *enters, using a pass key. He is carrying a tray of fresh fruit. He is the* HOTEL MANAGER.

MAN: Knock, knock.

GANESHA: Who's there?

MAN: Mahatma.

GANESHA: Mahatma who?

MAN: Mahatma Gandhi!

(They roar with laughter)

GANESHA: Very good, Mr. Biswas, very droll! *(To us)* Humor does not travel well. Especially Indian humor. "You had to be there" is, I believe, your word for it. Well, five words actually. You have to be here, I'm afraid.

MAN: What are you watching?

GANESHA: "The Ramayana." It's very sad. Valmiki's wife is dying. She's sent for their firstborn to bless him before she dies. My husband says I cry at everything.

MAN: The actress playing her has fine breasts. Do you know what they call them in Boston? Jugs. The actress playing her has very fine jugs. *(Phone stops ringing but* MAN *picks it up anyway)* Hello? Hello? *(He hangs up)* Bloody phone system. Bloody Third World. Bloody India. Why is it so dark in here? Are they here?

GANESHA: The nice one.

MAN: Mrs. Brynne?

GANESHA: Mrs. Civil.

MAN (calling out): Hello? Bonjour? Guttentag, Mrs. Civil!

GANESHA: She's in the bathroom being sick.

MAN: That's how most of them see India. Staring at the bottom of a toilet bowl. Tell me, Mrs. Jog, would you fly half way around the world and spend all your husband's money, just to heave your guts up for a fortnight in a country you have no way of understanding? I've seen this episode. It's a bloody rerun!

MARGARET (off): Yes? Is someone out there? Kitty? Is that you?

MAN: Some fruit, madam, compliments of the Lake Palace Hotel. Welcome to Udaipur!

MARGARET (off): What? I can't hear!

MAN: Let me open your shutters. You have a wonderful view here. (He throws open the shutters. Enormous light change. The gauze backdrop begins to sway in a delicious breezing coming in from the lake) Lord, but it takes my breath away every time, Mrs. Jog! You can say bloody this and bloody that, Mr. Victor Biswas, but you can never say bloody that.

(MARGARET comes into the room. She is in a robe and looks very pale)

MARGARET: Yes? Can I help you?

MAN (singing, but not well): "There she is, Miss America!" Welcome to the lake city of Udaipur, known as the City of the Sunrise, a cool oasis in the dry heart of Rajasthan, scene of a delightful episode in "Jewel in the Crown" and the exciting submarine/helicopter chase sequence in the most excellent James Bond motion picture "You

Only Live Once." Mr. Sean Connery himself occupied this very
room.

MARGARET: Really!

GANESHA: "Twice. You Only Live *Twice.*" You said "You Only Live
Once."

MAN: Shut up. (*To* MARGARET) The maid wants to know if she can get
you anything?

MARGARET: No, thank you. I just want to be still for a little while. I'm a
bit weak. It's so bright in here.

MAN: The way the sun hits the water. The Moghuls used to tie their
prisoners to stakes and sew their eyelids open and make them look
at the water until they went blind or mad or both.

MARGARET: How horrible!

MAN: We were conquered by a very cruel people. I hope you will find
that very little of that cruelty remains. (*To* GANESHA) What are you
looking at?

GANESHA: I like hearing you speak English, Mr. Biswas. I am in awe of
people who can speak with other people in a language not their
own. That is a God-like thing to be able to do.

MAN (*to* MARGARET): The maid is saying she likes to hear me speak
English. (*To* GANESHA) Why? You don't understand. If you did, you
would know I am telling this rich American lady what a lazy,
worthless worker you are and that you are this close to being made
redundant. Now clean room 617. Mr. Thomas had an accident on
the sheets last night.

GANESHA: Please, don't make me redundant, Mr. Biswas. I need this
job.

MAN: Then don't ever correct me again. Especially in front of a woman. (*To* MARGARET): She's saying she hopes you enjoy your stay with us. Her name is Queenie.

MARGARET: Thank you, Queenie.

(GANESHA *heads for the door just as* KATHARINE *returns.* KATHARINE *has been shopping. She has packages. She is out of breath but very excited*)

KATHARINE: Offamof! Off-a-mof! Is that our view? (*She stands by the open window*)

MAN: This is our very finest accommodation.

KATHARINE: Well, sir, as my grandchildren would say: OFF-A-FUCK-ING-MOFF! The things I've seen and done this morning! You people have Bombay knocked into a cocked hat! (*To* MARGARET) How are you feeling?

MARGARET: Much better.

KATHARINE: You sure? You had me worried. Poor baby.

MARGARET: This is Mr. Biswas, the hotel manager.

MAN: Victor Biswas. At your service, madam.

KATHARINE: Hello. I can see some color in her cheeks. Thank God! We have a train to catch this evening. (*She makes a quick sign of the Cross*) Whew! I've been shopping my tits off, Margaret. (*She finally sits*)

MAN: Tits? Are they like jugs, Mrs. Brynne?

KATHARINE: I think they're a little more contemporary than jugs, Mr. Biswas.

MAN: I am also puzzling over your curious expression, "off-a-mof." The adjective you embellished it with I understood quite clearly.

KATHARINE: It's short for "O for a Muse of fire," which is Shakespeare and which I say when I get excited and can't describe things and since I'm excited a lot lately, Mrs. Civil can't stand me saying it all the time and out of deference to her I shortened it to "offamof."

MAN: I see.

KATHARINE: "Thank you, Kitty." "*De nada, Margaret.*" I didn't buy that much. It just looks like it. I spent fifty dollars, tops.

MAN: I hope you find everything you are looking for in our country, including good bargains. I come home burdened down with VCRs and Calvin Klein underwear whenever I visit yours. Excuse me. We have a busload of Japs arriving. (*He goes*)

KATHARINE: Did you hear that? He said Japs.

MARGARET: He doesn't know better. Besides, it's not his first language.

KATHARINE (*to* GANESHA): Queenie, did you wash and iron my blouse?

GANESHA: Yes, Mrs. Brynne.

KATHARINE: *Ladesh.* (*To* MARGARET) That's Hindi for "thank you." (*To* GANESHA) *Ladesh, Queenie, ladesh.*

GANESHA: *De nada, Mrs. Brynne.* (*He goes*)

KATHARINE: Did you hear that, too, Margaret?

MARGARET: I heard, Kitty.

KATHARINE (*sticking her tongue out at her*): I'm sorry. I couldn't resist. I'll shut up. It's the heat, I'm delirious, all this talk about Calvin Klein underwear! Do you want to see what I bought?

(*She will show her purchases to* MARGARET *during the following*)

MARGARET: Kitty, what do you think a man like Mr. Biswas thinks when you say something like "shop your tits off"?

KATHARINE: I don't know. I don't care. I'm in India. I'm just your basic white trash, Margaret. You like these?

MARGARET: Don't be ridiculous.

KATHARINE: It's true. You are traveling with a woman whose father was a postal clerk and whose mother did ironing. I thought this blue bag would be for Linda Nagle.

MARGARET: Your father worked in a post office?

KATHARINE: For twenty-two years. He dropped dead selling Mrs. Feigen a three-cents stamp. Remember them? I was still in school. I did a little ironing myself after that. I think these are absolutely stunning, don't you? Only two dollars!

MARGARET: I had no idea, Kitty. Not that it matters.

KATHARINE: Oh, it matters, Margaret. Eventually, it matters. I have no class.

MARGARET: Don't say things like that.

KATHARINE: It's true.

MARGARET: Don't even think them. You and George have a wonderful life.

KATHARINE: I suppose we do but it's not what I'm talking about. I think these will make darling luncheon napkins. You know how I met him? I crashed a dance at the Westchester Country Club. My best friend and I, Flo Sullivan, we made ourselves fancy evening dresses and hiked our skirts up and carried our shoes and we walked across the wet grass on the golf course and snuck into the party through the terrace. The ballroom was so beautiful! Roses everywhere. Real ones. A mirror ball. Guy Lombardo was playing.

Himself, no substitute but the real thing. This was a class affair, right down the line. Guy Lombardo and His Royal Canadians. "Begin The Beguine." I knew right away this was where I wanted to be and I would do everything I could to stay there. I would scratch, I would fight, I would bite. Barbara Stanwyck was my role model. George was in white tie and tails, if you can imagine him in such a thing. He had a silver cigarette case and was tapping one end of his cigarette against it to get the tobacco down. I thought it was the most elegant gesture I'd ever seen a man make. (*Lights up on* MAN. *He is* GEORGE, *dressed in white tie and tails and tapping a cigarette against a silver case. He will dance to the music* KATHARINE *has described*) We hit it off right away. I was a wonderful dancer. I'd made sure of that. I knew how to let the man think he was leading. With George I didn't have to. I knew he was going to ask me where I went to college. What I didn't know was what I was going to answer. When he did, it was during a Lindy. I closed my eyes, held my breath and jumped. "I graduated Port Chester High School and I'm working in the city as a dental assistant." "Great," he said. "I was afraid you were going to say you went to Vassar!" and laughed and lifted me up by the waist over his head for this incredibly long second, like we were two colored kids jitterbugging in Harlem and I felt a blaze of happiness, like I've never felt before or since! After two hours, I said, "Let me wear your class ring. For fun. We'll pretend." It was a Yale ring. I showed it to Flo in the ladies room during a band break. She couldn't believe it. She asked if she could try it on. I was washing my hands and it slipped out of my fingers and disappeared down the drain. What do you tell a man you just met two hours ago at a dance you crashed when you've lost his senior class ring? You don't tell him very much, Maggie. You sleep with him on the first date and you say "I do," after you make sure he asks you to bury him on the third. I mean, marry him. I can't believe I said that. Bury him. This is my favorite. (*She is holding out a small carved figure*)

MARGARET: What an extraordinary story. You never told me that.

KATHARINE: "Hi, I'm Katharine Brynne. I met my husband crashing a dance at the Westchester Country Club." I don't think so, Margaret. Do you know who that is? It's Ganesha.

(MARGARET *examines the carving. Lights up on* MAN. *He is* WALTER. *He is unbloodied*)

MAN: May I have this dance, Miss Stanwyck? Oh, come on, it's only me. It's a slow fox trot. Your favorite kind.

(He holds his arms out to her)

KATHARINE: Since when do you like to dance with women?

MAN: I don't. I'll suffer. (*She joins him*) Besides, you're not a woman. You're my mother.

(They begin to dance. There is music)

KATHARINE: Go ahead. Say it. Criticize. Everything I do is wrong.

MAN: How could you tell that story to a total stranger and not your own son?

KATHARINE: She's not a total stranger. Besides, you wouldn't have understood.

MAN: No, I would have understood. That's what you were afraid of. That's the kind of story that makes you like someone. We might have become friends over a story like that.

MARGARET: He —I guess it's a he; in this day and age, I better watch what I say— he/she/it's got the head of an elephant.

KATHARINE: You wouldn't have approved, Walter.

MAN: You think Mrs. Civil does? (*He laughs*) God, I was a judgmental little shit where you and Dad were concerned.

KATHARINE: Serves us right. Well, me certainly. So am I still your best girl? Your *numero uno?*

MAN: I don't think we're supposed to say things like that.

KATHARINE: So sue me. That's from "Guys and Dolls."

MAN: "Shut up and dance." That's from "Gypsy."

MARGARET: It looks like he's got four arms. I'm sure it's a he. Six arms? No, four. Definitely four.

MAN: This is a long song.

KATHARINE: We can stop.

MAN: I'm too much of a gentleman.

MARGARET: What's that around his waist? A snake! A cobra. And one of his tusks is broken.

(Lights up on GANESHA. *He is on a platform and holds his broken tusk in his right hand)*

GANESHA: I broke it off one night and threw it at the moon because she made me angry by laughing at me.

KATHARINE: You still don't know how to hold a woman.

MAN: You mean, like this? *(He pulls her to him hard and close)* Is this how you mean?

(She slaps him)

KATHARINE: I'm sorry. I'm sorry.

MAN: No, you're not.

MARGARET *(approaching him)*: May I cut in?

MAN: Thank you. *(They begin to dance)* Do I know you?

MARGARET: No, Gabriel.

KATHARINE: Break her heart, the way you did mine. I hate you. I hate both of you!

MAN: Who are you?

MARGARET: Never mind. I just want to dance with you. I have always wanted to dance with you.

GANESHA (*to* KATHARINE): Join me. With worshippers at my feet I dance my swaying dance. Come, join us!

KATHARINE: Who are you?

GANESHA: I am Ganesha, a very important god in India. Don't laugh. Just because I'm fat and have the head of an elephant doesn't mean that I'm not a god of great influence and popularity. They call me "The Lord of Obstacles." I am good at overcoming problems and bringing success to people. I am also known as a god of wisdom and wealth.

MARGARET: You're a wonderful dancer.

MAN: Thank you.

MARGARET: I'm not. You don't have to say anything.

MAN: I wasn't going to. Hang on!

(*This time he will whirl her wildly*)

MARGARET: Oh, Gabriel!

(*They are gone*)

KATHARINE: I think you're darling. Ganesh!

GANESHA: Or Ganesha. It's all the same to me.

KATHARINE: I like Ganesh. Tell me more. I want to know everything about you.

GANESHA: Because I'm a god, I don't have to look or do things the way ordinary people do. For instance, as you can plainly see, I have an elephant's head. You don't. You travel by Ford Escort or on foot. I ride a rat. It may seem strange for a great big fellow like me to have such a small vehicle, but I find him very helpful for getting out of tight situations. He's almost always with me but sometimes hard to find. Look for him carefully.

KATHARINE: I see him! I see the rat!

GANESHA: This demonstrates the concept —so important to me!— that opposites —an elephant and a mouse— can live together happily. That love of good food (I am always eating) and profound spiritual knowledge can go together. That a fat, rotund person can still be a supreme connoisseur of dance and music. In fact, I prove that the world is full of opposites which exist peacefully side by side.

KATHARINE: You can stop right there. I'm sold. Do you come any smaller? I couldn't possibly lug you back to Connecticut like that.

GANESHA: Let me check for you.

(*Lights fade on* GANESHA *as* MARGARET *and* MAN *appear again, still dancing.* KATHARINE *watches them.* MAN *whispers something in* MARGARET'S *ear. She throws her head back and laughs*)

KATHARINE: May I cut in?

MARGARET: No.

MAN: I'm sorry.

(*They dance away from her*)

MARGARET: Was that terrible of us?

MAN: Terribly! You're very beautiful.

MARGARET: Thank you.

MAN: For your years.

MARGARET: Did you have to say that?

MAN: Are you happy?

(He stops dancing)

MARGARET *(wanting to resume)*: Yes. No. I don't know. Does it matter? Are you? Please, don't look at me like that.

(He kisses her)

MAN: You should be happy.

MARGARET: I can't be.

MAN: I never knew what hit me. *(He snaps his fingers)* Like that. *(He goes)*

(Lights up on GANESHA. *He approaches* KATHARINE *with a small carving of himself)*

GANESHA: Is this small enough, excellent lady? *(He hands it to* KATHARINE*)* I come key-ring and necklace pendant size, too, but when I get that small I only come in plastic and you lose all the detail.

KATHARINE: Excuse me, did you say "I?" "I only come in plastic"?

GANESHA: Oh, Lordy, no! That would be a blasphemy.

KATHARINE: This one is perfect. What's it made of?

GANESHA: I believe that's amethyst but let me check. Solar! My wife has all the answers. Solar!

KATHARINE: How much?

GANESHA: Fifty rupees?

KATHARINE: I'll take two. My friend, Mrs. Civil, is back in our hotel room writhing in agony. Her stomach. Montezuma's Revenge they call it in Mexico. What do you call it here?

GANESHA: Just dysentery. We have no sense of humor when it comes to the bowels.

KATHARINE: Margaret would say, "That's something"!

GANESHA: You must not drink our water. Or eat our fruit. No matter how tempting.

KATHARINE: She didn't.

GANESHA: That's what you all say.

KATHARINE: But she didn't!

GANESHA: Solar!

(He goes)

KATHARINE: I'm hoping this will cheer her up! (*She looks down at the carving in her hand. So does* MARGARET) Isn't he darling? Maybe he'll help me get back that camera I lost in Jodhpur. George is going to kill me.

MARGARET (*reading*): "I'm happy and I want people to be happy, too." Thank you, Kitty.

KATHARINE: I'm just glad you're better. You're going to miss India at this rate. The Towers of Silence were the highlight of Bombay —unforgettable!— and you completely missed them.

MARGARET: I thought you couldn't see them.

KATHARINE: No, I said you just couldn't see the vultures actually eating the flesh off the bones, if that's what you're talking about. You have to be a Parsi. But you could stand outside looking up at the towers and see the vultures swooping down on the bodies on top. That was quite enough for this cookie, thank you very much. Talk about feeling mortal. That could have been me up there! One day it will be. When I go, that's what I want done, Margaret. Just leave me out on the pier at the Greenwich Yacht Club and let the seagulls go to work. (*The telephone begins to ring wanly again*) I'm not even going to answer it anymore. I'm glad you like him. I thought you would. (*The sounds of a train have gotten quite loud*)

MARGARET: I just want to know why he has a head for an elephant?

KATHARINE: What?

MARGARET: I mean, why he has an elephant's head?

KATHARINE: What? I can't hear you!

(*Transition as sounds level out to:*)

Scene Two

The Palace on Wheels, India's legendary luxury train. Teatime. MARGA-
RET, KATHARINE *and the* MAN. *The* MAN *is an* AUTHORITY. *He is examining a
figure of Ganesh.*

MARGARET: I wish they kept these windows cleaner. How are we supposed to see anything! How's your side?

KATHARINE: The same.

MARGARET: I told you to take Pepto Bismol.

MAN (*returning the Ganesh*): It's soapstone.

KATHARINE: They said it was amethyst.

MAN: I'm surprised he didn't tell you it was marble. That's their usual
ploy, God love 'em. No, it's soapstone. I'm afraid they saw you
coming, Mrs. Brynne.

MARGARET: That's what I told her. Maybe she'll listen to you.

KATHARINE: I don't care what he's made of. I love him.

MARGARET: Kitty's become besotted with this Ganesh/Ganesha person.

KATHARINE: He's not a person. He's a God. And I'm not besotted with
him.

MARGARET: I'm just hoping someone will tell us how he got his elephant's head.

MAN: It's a dreadful story. I don't think Mrs. Brynne wants to hear it
on that stomach of hers.

KATHARINE: I'm fine.

MAN: Let's get some tea first. (*He rings*) So you two ladies have fallen under the spell of Ganesha, too? Most travelers to India do. My first trip I couldn't get enough of him. I started developing this lump in the middle of my forehead. A sort of psychosomatic trunk.

KATHARINE: He's kidding, Margaret.

MARGARET: I know that. I knew that.

KATHARINE: I'm not besotted. I'm curious. I don't think Mrs. Civil is enjoying India.

MARGARET: That's not true.

KATHARINE: I adore it, of course.

MAN: Hindu mythology is so violent. It gives me the creeps. I'll settle for a hammer and nails, your basic wooden cross and a nice Jewish boy. I hope I haven't offended anyone.

KATHARINE: Just about everyone.

MAN: You two are a trip. I'm so glad I ran into you.

KATHARINE: Why thank you, kind sir! You should see me when my guts don't feel like someone has got their hands in there and is tying them in knots.

MARGARET: She'd be dancing on the table.

MAN (*to* KATHARINE): You know, you remind me of someone: my mother.

KATHARINE: Ow! Such cramps. Out of the blue. Just when you think they've—! Ow! Ow! Ow!

MARGARET: I told her: Don't eat that papaya.

KATHARINE: It wasn't a papaya! I thought peeling it would make it safe.

(GANESH *appears. He carries a tray*)

MAN: Tea for three, please. Understand? Tea for three.

KATHARINE: *Ladesh.*

MARGARET (*anticipating what* KATHARINE *will say*): "That's Hindi for 'thank you'."

KATHARINE (*to* MAN): That's Hindi for "thank you."

MARGARET: What did I tell you?

MAN: My wife would get such a kick out of you two!

KATHARINE: I can't believe she just flew home without you.

MAN: She couldn't take India. A lot of people can't. Too much poverty, too much disease.

KATHARINE: Too much everything. The colors, the smells, the sounds. My head is whirling, when my stomach isn't heaving.

MARGARET: Our husbands wouldn't even consider coming with us. "No way, José" was how Alan put it.

MAN: Actually, we had an incident in Benares. Are you going there?

KATHARINE: Absolutely. Benares is one of the reasons I most wanted to come to India.

MARGARET: You never told me that.

KATHARINE: What happened?

MAN: I don't want to upset you or anything and I'm sure this won't happen to you, but we were down at the ghats where they burn the bodies. I've always been terrified of death and I thought maybe just looking at it would help. Hundreds of dead bodies being burned like so many logs. Who knew? Maybe it *would* help and besides, people like us, we don't go to Benares without seeing the burning ghats, am I right?

KATHARINE: Go on.

MAN: They were burning the body of an old woman. I wish I could say I thought it was beautiful or spiritual but I thought it was horrible and it scared the shit out of me. Kelly was holding my hand so tight I thought she would puncture my flesh with her nails. Suddenly, someone called out behind us. A harsh, ugly sound. We turned and this wretched figure in rags on the ground was pointing at us and yelling. We started to run but Kelly tripped, I lost my grip on her, and she fell on top of him. When their bodies hit, he somehow seemed to throw his arms around her, hug her almost, and they rolled over and over in the mud. I couldn't pull them apart. Kelly was screaming but he wouldn't let go. Finally, it seemed like forever, two policemen appeared and they pulled him off her and apologized and then hit the old man with their truncheons and escorted us back to our hotel.

MARGARET: You're not going to the burning ghats!

MAN: I don't know if he was a leper, Kelly says he was, but she did say, "I will never, ever be clean again. I know it." She took shower after shower after shower but nothing would convince her that she was rid of him: his smell, his dirt, his essence, I suppose. I haven't heard from her since she got back to Boston. Poor baby. Let's hope.

KATHARINE: You didn't think of going back with her?

MAN: We don't have that sort of marriage. No children and we're very independent.

KATHARINE: But still . . .

MAN: I don't expect other people to understand. Besides, being in India is rather a solo project, anyway. It's finally just you and it.

(GANESHA *has returned with the tea*) Thank you. (*To* KATHARINE) What was that word?

KATHARINE: *Ladesh.*

MAN: *Ladesh.*

(*The compartment suddenly goes dark. The train has entered a tunnel*)

MARGARET: What happened!

KATHARINE: It's just a tunnel.

MAN: A long one, ladies. You haven't read your guide books. The Chittaurgahr Pass. The longest tunnel in India. Nearly 42 kilometers.

MARGARET: What is that in miles?

MAN: I don't know. Thirty-five miles or so.

KATHARINE: If this were a movie, one of us would have a dagger in his back when he came out of it!

MAN: Or been kissed or pinched or both.

KATHARINE: You have a romantic imagination.

MAN: And you have a morbid one!

KATHARINE: You were going to tell us how Ganesh got his elephant's head.

MAN: All right, but I warned you.

MARGARET: Are we really going to be in a dark tunnel for the next hour?

KATHARINE: We're fine, Margaret. Nothing's going to happen.

MARGARET: Palace on Wheels! Dungeon on Wheels is more like it.

KATHARINE: Ignore her. Go ahead.

MARGARET: There was a dead spider in my bed last night.

MAN: Where was I?

MARGARET: I won't even go into the food!

MAN: Oh, Ganesha's head!

MARGARET: Oh! That wasn't funny.

KATHARINE: What?

MARGARET: Whoever did that, I didn't appreciate it.

(GANESH *strikes a match and lights a kerosene lamp for them*)

MAN: *Ladesh. Ladesh.*

KATHARINE: What's the matter, Margaret?

MARGARET: Someone . . . I distinctly felt a hand . . .

KATHARINE: What?

MARGARET: On my breast. Someone . . . touched it . . .

KATHARINE: Margaret.

MARGARET: I'm sure of it.

KATHARINE: Was it a friendly hand?

MARGARET: I'm serious.

KATHARINE: I'm sure whatever it was —if it was anything— just felt like a hand.

MARGARET: I guess I still know what a hand on my breast feels like, Katharine, even if you don't remember.

KATHARINE: What is that supposed to mean?

MARGARET: I think you know.

GANESHA: Is there something wrong? The lady seems agitated.

MARGARET: What's he saying?

GANESHA: The tea was not good? I shall bring more candles?

MARGARET: I didn't accuse him. I don't know what he's babbling about.

(GANESH *is in a dither*)

KATHARINE: Well, who else were you accusing?

MAN: I can assure you, Mrs. Civil, grabbing women's breasts in dark railway tunnels is not my thing.

MARGARET: I didn't say it was.

MAN: And I doubt it was our porter. He's gay as a goose, can't you tell?

GANESHA (*with a napkin*): Crumbs on the lady! Here, let me—!

(*He moves to brush off her chest with his serving napkin.* MARGARET *pushes him away*)

MARGARET: No!

GANESHA: I have done something wrong? I have given offense?

MAN: Fine! Everything is fine!

MARGARET: Everything is not fine.

KATHARINE: Now who's the Ugly American!

MARGARET: This isn't about that, Kitty.

KATHARINE: And I won't forget that remark about George.

MARGARET: What remark?

KATHARINE: He touches me just fine! What would you know about it?

MAN: Ladies, please!

GANESHA: The lady is frightened of the tunnel? Tell the lady there is nothing to fear. See? I laugh at the tunnel. Ha ha ha!

KATHARINE: What is he doing?

GANESHA: Ha ha ha!

MAN: Go! Go back to where you came from!

GANESHA: Ganesha loves you. Ganesha will protect you.

KATHARINE: Wait! He said something about Ganesha. Did you say Ganesha?

GANESHA (*joyfully*): Ganesha, yes, Ganesha!

KATHARINE: There, hear that? He said Ganesha.

MARGARET: I suppose Ganesha fondled my breast!

GANESHA: Ganesha! Ganesha!

KATHARINE: Now it's "fondled." First it was just "touched." Next we'll be having the Marabar Caves incident.

GANESHA (*fearfully*): Marabar! No, no! No, Marabar!

KATHARINE: I'm not accusing you!

GANESHA: No, Marabar! Bad, Marabar! You wrong! No, Marabar! I am
going to my supervisor and tell him the truth before you ladies lie
and have Anant made redundant. Marabar, no! (*He goes*)

KATHARINE: What did I say? Rather, what did he think I said?

MAN: The one porter in all Rajasthan who's read *Passage to India.*

MARGARET: I'm glad you find this so amusing.

KATHARINE: No one finds it amusing, Margaret, but we can't go around
accusing people because we feel superior to them.

MARGARET: I don't feel superior to that person.

KATHARINE: Yes, you do. So do I. And by our standards, we are. That's
the terrible thing.

MARGARET: Spare us this, Kitty.

MAN: If you ladies will excuse me, but I've already done this part with
Kelly.

KATHARINE: We're sorry.

MAN: I saw a three–month–old copy of the *Village Voice* with a review
of Bob Dylan at the Garden in the library. Or what Indian Rail
calls the library. Bob Dylan! God, we're all getting so old. (*He goes*)

MARGARET: No, he doesn't remind me of Walter either.

KATHARINE: I wasn't going to say that.

MARGARET: There is evil in the world, Katharine.

KATHARINE: I know that.

MARGARET: And I was just subjected to some of it.

KATHARINE: So was my son.

MARGARET: Do you want to cut the trip short?

KATHARINE: No. Do you?

MARGARET: No. (*Long pause. The sound of the train gets louder and louder*) I'm sorry.

KATHARINE: It's all right. So am I. So am I. (*Suddenly the train comes out of the tunnel and the light will seem very bright*) I thought he said we'd be in there for an hour.

MARGARET: That type thinks they know everything.

KATHARINE: I thought you liked him.

MARGARET: I did, for fifteen minutes. Look, there's some nice scenery coming up. (*They look out the window on different sides of the compartment*) I like everyone for fifteen minutes.

KATHARINE: Thank you.

MARGARET: Don't be ridiculous. You're my oldest friend.

KATHARINE: We hardly know each other.

MARGARET: That's not true. We know each other. We love each other. We just don't especially like each other. I've got water buffaloes on my side. What do you have?

KATHARINE: Camels.

MARGARET: I would imagine people had this same view thousands of years ago, before electricity, before television and atomic bombs, before we all got so neurotic. You were born, you grew up, you worked in a field like those, you got married, you had children, you got old, you died and with a little luck, somebody remembered you kindly for at least one generation.

KATHARINE: I don't feel like I'm in India. I see sky and hills and horizon and trees. What makes it India and not Danbury? We travel, but we don't go anywhere. I'm stuck right here. The earth spins but I don't.

(GANESHA *appears in the compartment. He is a Supervisor*)

GANESHA: Excuse me, ladies, I understand there was some disturbance here? Some confusion?

MARGARET: No, nothing, we're fine. We're both fine.

KATHARINE: Yes, thank you.

GANESHA: But I was told—

MARGARET: Really, it's quite forgotten. When are we getting to Jaipur?

GANESHA: At exactly 23:30. In time for the fireworks and the great Hali Festival.

KATHARINE: I have a feeling we won't be three for dinner this evening.

GANESHA: Ah, yes, the gentleman already explained that. Goodbye then. (*He goes*)

MARGARET: I wish I could be a better friend to you, Kitty, and vice versa. I don't know what stops me.

KATHARINE: Thank you for not making an issue about your breast.

MARGARET: It's that good Yankee breeding, don't you know. It's all in the genes and we all have these marvelous cheekbones and talk

like Katharine Hepburn. We're both the same age and we're from
the same background—

KATHARINE: Or so you thought!

MARGARET: Our husbands make approximately the same living. We're
both mothers.

KATHARINE: You never lost a child.

MARGARET: Well, that's true.

KATHARINE: Nothing compares to losing a child. No, nothing compares
to losing that particular child. Why couldn't it have been his
brother or Nan or one of her kids or George even? Do you think
God will strike me dead for saying something like that?

MARGARET: Of course not.

KATHARINE: I think maybe he should. Every time the phone rang I
dreaded it being him and him saying, "Mom, I've got it. I've got
AIDS."

MARGARET: You want to talk about it?

KATHARINE: What is there to say? Who the hell are you to tell me
there's evil in the world? You think some little brown man touched
your tit in a tunnel. I'm surprised the earth didn't spin off its axis! I
know what one, two, three, four, five, six —count 'em: six!— Afri-
can-Americans did to my son at two-thirty in the morning at the
corner of Barrow and Greenwich. They get off (Walter was a faggot
after all!) and I don't even get to say nigger! I know there's evil. I'm
not so sure there's any justice.

MARGARET: I wish I could comfort you.

KATHARINE: I wish you could, too. Now I've got the water buffaloes.

MARGARET: May I put my arm around you?

KATHARINE: I'd rather you wouldn't.

MARGARET (*putting her arm around her*): You don't have to say anything. Sshh! Sshh! I'm not going to say anything.

KATHARINE: Thank you for that, at least.

MARGARET: You're not alone, Kitty. I'm here. Another person, another woman, is here. Right here. Breathing the same air. Riding the same train. Looking out the window at the same timeless landscape. You are not alone. Even in your agony.

KATHARINE: Thank you.

MARGARET: I love you. I love you very much. "Offamof."

KATHARINE: What?

MARGARET: "Offamof."

KATHARINE: Oh, yeah, "Offamof"!

(*Lights up on* GANESHA. *He comes down to us as the sounds of the train come up and the lights dim on* MARGARET *and* KATHARINE)

GANESHA: And so it happened that while Margaret Civil and Katharine Brynne stared with heavy, sad, sad eyes at what Mr. Ray of India Rail injudiciously called the most beautiful scenery in India, some 8,345 miles away, at 11:20 p.m. their time, George Brynne, Katharine Brynne's husband, Caucasian male, aged 62, lost control of his car on a patch of something called glare ice on his way home from a movie Katharine had refused to see because of its purported violence (she was right! an appalling motion picture it was, too!), went into a skid and slammed into a 300-year-old oak tree. He died instantly. Mrs. Brynne will not learn of her loss until she gets home. Since her children cannot reach her by phone (the ladies are off their itinerary and frequently without reservations; in Khajuraho they slept on two cots in the garden of a sympathetic postmaster), her children decide it is better to meet her at the airport when she and Mrs. Civil return.

(Lights are coming up on MARGARET *and* KATHARINE. *The sounds of the train have faded. We hear the periodic ringing of a temple bell)*

MARGARET: I can't believe you've actually lost your guidebook, Kitty.

KATHARINE: Sooner or later, I lose everything.

MARGARET: How are you going to know what you're looking at?

KATHARINE: I am putting myself completely in the hands of our guide, Mr. Kamlesh Tandu of Jodhpur.

GANESHA *(to us)*: I think Mrs. Brynne has a slight "thing" for me, I believe you call them. It's very curious but not uncommon. In her own country she wouldn't give me the time of day.

MARGARET: Well don't come running to me when we leave Mr. Tandu in Jaiselmir and you want to know what something is. I'm not going to tell you.

KATHARINE: As Rudyard Kipling said, "Oh, bugger off, Margaret!"

MARGARET: I'm sure Rudyard Kipling never said "Bugger off, Margaret." Somerset Maugham maybe.

GANESHA *(stepping forward)*: Welcome to my humble village, lovely ladies. No television, no electricity. Puppet shows and traveling players are our windows on the world. It's lovely.

KATHARINE: You said you had a treat for us, Mr. Tandu.

GANESHA: No, for you, Mrs. Brynne. That is if you don't mind, Mrs. Civil.

MARGARET: Not in the least.

KATHARINE: Why just for me?

GANESHA: Why not? (*clapping hands*) Puppets, please.

Scene Three

A village square. Dusk. A puppet show is in progress. The MAN *is a* PUPPETEER. *There are three camp stools for* MARGARET, KATHARINE *and* GANESHA.

GANESHA: Once again, lovely ladies, "How Ganesha Got His Lovely Elephant's Head." Puppets, please. (*He has handed her a small book*)

KATHARINE: What's this?

GANESHA: Your part. In India we participate in theatre. We don't sit back, arms folded and say "Show me."

(MARGARET *has been sitting exactly like that*)

MARGARET: I'm sorry.

KATHARINE: "Still in a fury because his wife would not see him, Shiva sent his armies to kill the boy who barred his way."

GANESHA: Very good!

KATHARINE: "But Parvati created two shaktis to defend her son against her husband, Kali and Durga."

MAN (*showing the puppets*): Kali and Durga!

MARGARET: What's a shakti, Mr. Tandu?

GANESHA: I believe you call them She-devils, Mrs. Civil.

KATHARINE: No, we say bitches. Don't interrupt, Margaret. This is my

big moment. "To his amazement, Shiva's forces were completely
routed by the valiant youth. He knew what he must do."

MAN: "I will have to kill the boy with my own hands. Let it never be
said that a man was subservient to his wife!"

MARGARET: That sounds familiar.

KATHARINE: "Shiva charged the boy with his silver-shining trident but
the boy swung his iron club and sent him sprawling." Good for the
boy!

MAN: "That should teach you a lesson, old man, pop."

KATHARINE (*looking up from the book*): What?

MAN (*to* KATHARINE): "Mother, see how I serve you."

(*From this point,* KATHARINE *will not be able to take her eyes off the
puppets and the* MAN. *She will let the playbook lie open in her lap*)

GANESHA: And the boy laughed. Oh, how he laughed!

MAN: Ha ha ha! Ha ha ha!

MARGARET: Ha ha ha! Ha ha ha! This is charming.

GANESHA: And while the boy laughed, Shiva came up from behind him
and with one swift stroke of his sword, cut off Walter's head.

MAN: Whoosh. Ung.

GANESHA: He could hear the sound against the side of his head.

MAN: Whoosh. Ung.

GANESHA: Shiva had landed a good one. You're not looking, Mrs.
Brynne.

MAN: I stayed on my feet a remarkably long time, Mama. I was sort of proud of me.

KATHARINE (*looking back to the book*): Where does it say that?

MAN: "Mother, see how I serve you."

KATHARINE: He's not following the script.

GANESHA: And down he fell.

KATHARINE: Why me, Mr. Tandu?

GANESHA: Again, why not you, Mrs. Brynne? As the boy lay dying, Shiva realized what he had done.

KATHARINE: Shiva, not I! (*She abruptly stands up*)

MARGARET: Where are you going?

GANESHA: You must hear the story to its end, Mrs. Brynne.

KATHARINE: I know how it ends. In a New York hospital. Twenty minutes before I got there.

GANESHA: No, it ends in reconciliation, renewal and re-birth.

KATHARINE: Tell it to Mrs. Civil.

(*She hands the playbook to* MARGARET *and goes*)

MARGARET: I think your story upset Mrs. Brynne.

GANESHA: Perhaps she needed upsetting, Mrs. Civil. May we continue? It is very bad form to abandon Lord Ganesha in mid-stream. Shiva went to his wife and begged forgiveness for what he had done.

MAN: "O, great goddess, wife and mother forgive me."

GANESHA: Parvati faced him with great dignity. That's you, Mrs. Civil.

MARGARET: "I will. But my son must regain his life, and he must have an honorable status among you."

GANESHA: Lord Shiva responded with great humility.

MAN: "Your will shall be done. Vishnu, go north. Bring the head of the first creature that crosses your path. Fit that head to the boy's body and it will come to life."

MARGARET: And the first creature they saw was an elephant! With a single tusk!

GANESHA: Vishnu threw his golden discus and killed him.

MARGARET: And they cut off his head and fitted it to the body of her little boy.

GANESHA: The boy sat up.

MARGARET: He was reborn.

MAN: Then Shiva placed his hand on the boy's head and pronounced these solemn and healing words.

GANESHA: "Even as a mere boy, you showed great valor. You shall be Ganesha, the presiding officer of all my ganas. You shall be worthy of worship forever."

MAN: Mighty is the Lord Shiva, great is his compassion.

GANESHA: Here ends the lovely story of how Lord Ganesha got his lovely head.

MARGARET: Thank you.

GANESHA: There are many others, Mrs. Civil, if the ladies are so inclined.

MARGARET: I don't think so. I'm worried about my friend.

GANESHA: I said something wrong perhaps?

MARGARET: It almost seemed deliberate.

GANESHA: It's only a legend. You Christians take everything so literally.

MARGARET: She had a son who . . .

GANESHA: Whose head was cut off? My, my, my! This New York City of yours must be a fearful place.

MARGARET: Don't be ridiculous. His head wasn't cut off. He was murdered.

MAN: I heard of a man who went there and they ate his toes they were so hungry.

MARGARET: Don't believe such stories. I assure you, it hasn't come to that.

MAN (*to* GANESHA, *unconvinced*): They sold his eyeballs for drug money.

MARGARET: You have a horrible imagination.

MAN: Thank you very much.

MARGARET: Work on your English. It wasn't a compliment. (*She starts walking in the opposite direction* KATHARINE *took*) Katharine!

GANESHA: Tonight they ride elephants to a banquet in a maharajah's palace and dine by torchlight. Uh, lordy, look at me! I have to dress. *Sayonara. Ciao.*

(*Lights fade on* MAN *and* GANESHA *while* MARGARET *and* KATHARINE *walk. Again, a turntable would be useful*)

MARGARET: "Kitty! Kitty!"

KATHARINE: God, leave me alone, woman. All of you. No more guides or puppets. No more India. I want to go home and forget I ever came here. I'm sick of your mythology. It's as false as ours. My son was not reborn. He died twenty minutes before I got to the hospital. His murderers never asked my forgiveness. You had it easy, Parvati. No honor has ever been made to me. I have my anger and nothing more. No love. No love at all.

MARGARET: Katharine! Kitty! Now where is she gone to? She'd lose herself and not just the train tickets if I didn't keep an eye on her. I'm ashamed to admit it but I never realized how dependent we are on the men. She won't admit that but it's true. This is the last time I go anywhere with anyone. I'm not a fellow traveler. I almost told her about Gabriel. It would have been such a tiny leap across that void between two people. "I lost a son too, Kitty." Six little words and I couldn't do it. "I lost a son too, Kitty." Kitty!

(KATHARINE *has started walking with* GANESHA)

KATHARINE: How old are you? Do you speak any English? 7 years old? 8? How old are you?

(MARGARET *has started walking with the* MAN. *He is a* FOREIGN TOURIST)

MARGARET: Dutch? We've been to Holland. Twice. You have wonderful museums there. The Rembrandt Museum, one of my favorites.

MAN: Yes, Rembrandt.

MARGARET: My favorite painting is by Rembrandt, only it's in London at the National Gallery.

MAN: London, yes?

KATHARINE: You have the dearest face! Oh God, I wish I knew your name. When I get back to America I would send you the biggest box of anything you wanted.

GANESHA: Are you from America? How old are you? Are you rich? Is there really a Rocky? Who is your leader there now?

KATHARINE: Slow down, slow down! I don't understand a word you're saying. I do not speak Hindi.

GANESHA: I like you.

KATHARINE: Where are we going? I'm letting you take me.

MARGARET: It's called "Woman Bathing."

MAN: Yes?

MARGARET: Well, in English it's called "Woman Bathing." I don't know what it's called in Dutch. Do you know it?

MAN: Yes, "Woman Bathing"?

MARGARET: It's just a woman wading in a river. She has her shift pulled up to her thighs. She's looking at herself in the reflection of the water. She's very pensive but very powerful, too. It's a dark painting, most Rembrandt is, but there's something about it. Her isolation. Her independence. Her strength. I'm terrible talking about art. Are you good at it?

MAN: Yes?

(*A bolt of blue fabric is rolled across the white floor of the stage. It is a river.* KATHARINE *and* MARGARET *will find themselves on different sides of it*)

MARGARET: Oh, look, there's a river here. Can we sit and bathe our feet?

MAN: Very nice. (*They sit*)

KATHARINE: So this is where you were leading me? What's this river called?

MARGARET: Kitty, hello! Kitty! There's my friend on the other side of the river.

KATHARINE: Hello! That's Mrs. Civil. She is my friend.

MARGARET: She can't hear us. Who's your little friend?

KATHARINE: Behave yourself, you two! What is she doing?

(MARGARET *has started wading in the river*)

MARGARET: "Woman Bathing" by Rembrandt!

MAN: "Woman Bathing," ah, yes! Ha ha ha.

KATHARINE: You're a happy little person, aren't you? What's your secret? Everyone in India seems so content. I'm sure that's not true but you seem to possess some inner calm or confidence that we don't. I bet if I put even one finger on your belly you'll fall over giggling like a little doughboy!

(*She touches* GANESHA *in the stomach and he falls over giggling. She will continue to tickle him awhile. He is enjoying himself enormously*)

MARGARET: Every time I go to London I visit it. But the last time I looked at it something strange and rather awful happened. Two museum guards were talking as if I weren't there. One was a man, more or less my age, talking to a much younger woman, whom I assume was Indian or from Pakistan. You know what he said to her? Right in front of me, as if I were invisible! "No one wants me anymore. I've had my day. It's gone now." I wish people wouldn't say such deeply personal things in public. It stayed with me our entire trip. It almost ruined my Rembrandt. This was five or six years ago. It just came back to me.

MAN: London. Father's sister, London.

MARGARET: "No one wants me anymore. I've had my day. It's gone now." Isn't that a terrible thing to say with a total stranger listening?

KATHARINE: They're going back. (*She waves and calls across to them*) I'll see you in the room.

MARGARET (*waving and calling*): Five o'clock! Drinks with the manager!

(MARGARET *and* MAN *withdraw.*

Light change suggests the passage of time. GANESHA's *head is lying in* KATHARINE'S *lap*)

KATHARINE: My little brown *bambino.* My nutmeg *Gesu.* What color is your skin? Coffee? That's not right either. What color is mine? Not white. Where do words come from? What do they mean?

GANESHA: Walter.

KATHARINE: What? I thought you said, "Walter."

GANESHA: Walter.

KATHARINE: You did! You did say Walter!

GANESHA: Walter.

KATHARINE: Walter must be a word in Hindi then! Yes? Tell me, what does it mean, Walter?

GANESHA (*laughing merrily*): Walter! Walter!

(*He suddenly throws his arms around her and holds her tight*)

KATHARINE: Does it mean laughter? It means something joyful! Something good! It must! Walter! Walter! (*She puts her hands to her mouth and calls across the lake*) Walter! Walter!!

GANESHA (*imitating her*): Walter! Walter!

(There is an echo)

ECHO: Walter! Walter!

(There is a silence as the echo dies away)

KATHARINE: It's gone.

GANESHA: Why have you stopped smiling?

(She kisses him fiercely)

KATHARINE: Stay this way forever. When you grow up, I won't like you.
I will hate you and fear you because of the color of your skin —just
as I hated and feared my son because he loved men. I won't tell
you this to your face but you will know it, just as he did and it will
sicken and diminish us both.

GANESHA: Why are you looking at me so intently? What do you want to
see?

KATHARINE: I came here to heal but I can't forgive myself. Maybe if I
shout out the names of my fear and hatred of you across this holy
river they will vanish, too, just as "Walter" did. Faggot. Queer. The
words keep sticking.

GANESHA *(trying to imitate her, like before)*: Faggot? Queer?

KATHARINE: A little boy says it better than you.

GANESHA: Faggot? Queer?

KATHARINE: Again.

GANESHA *(happily, for her approval)*: Faggot! Queer!

KATHARINE: Again!

GANESHA *(bigger)*: Faggot! Queer!

KATHARINE: Louder!

GANESHA: Faggot! Faggot! Queer! Queer!

KATHARINE: No, with hatred! Like they did: Fag! Queer! Cocksucker! Dead from AIDS queer meat!

GANESHA: Oh dear, oh dear!

KATHARINE: FAGGOT! FAGGOT! QUEER! QUEER! NIGGER!

(KATHARINE *begins to break down. In the silence, we hear only her sobs*)

ECHO: Faggot, faggot! Queer, queer! Walter!

KATHARINE: Walter. Forgive me.

(GANESHA *cradles* KATHARINE *at the bank of the river.*

MAN *has appeared as* WALTER. *He waves to* KATHARINE, *blows her a kiss and disappears*)

GANESHA: Foolish woman. You were holding a god in your arms.

(*Lights change.* KATHARINE *stays where she is.* GANESHA *picks up a long pole. He is a* BOATMAN. *Sounds of water lapping*)

MARGARET: We're coming! We're coming.

(MARGARET *enters, hair covered by a scarf. The* MAN *is with her. He is a* GUIDE.)

Scene Four

On the Ganges River in Varanasi. MARGARET, KATHARINE *and* MAN *sit in a small skiff, piloted by* GANESHA. *It is early morning and very misty.*

MARGARET: Look what you left in the room! We wouldn't have seen a thing. Thank God I went back for a scarf. (*She has a pair of binocu-lars*) Is someone going to give me a hand? (GANESHA *puts his hand out to her as she steps aboard the skiff. It threatens to capsize*) Oh my God! Is this safe? Are we all going to drown in the Ganges?

MAN: Not if you sit down, Mrs. Civil!

MARGARET: I can't sit down until it stops rocking.

GANESHA: She's going to make us capsize.

MAN: Grab the sides and sit!

(MARGARET *steadies herself and sits.* GANESHA *will help* MAN *aboard the skiff and then guide it out into the river*)

MARGARET: This is madness. I'm never going to see Pumpkin Fields Lane again. I hate you for doing this. I hate myself for coming.

MAN (*to* GANESH): Thank you.

MARGARET (*to* GANESHA): Oh, yes, thank you! (*Then*) Who would think to bring Dramamine to India? Dramamine is for when we take the QE2. Where's your scarf? Mr. Tennyson warned us about this damp morning air. You just got over dysentery. Next stop, pneumonia. Then on to God knows what!

KATHARINE: Margaret, please, sshh!

MARGARET: You're right, I'm sorry. I'll practice what they taught us at the yoga institute in Delhi. Om! It's not working. Don't mind me, everyone. They're not. That's what's so pathetic!

MAN: Benares, now called Varanasi, the "eternal city," is one of the most important pilgrimage sites in India and also a major tourist attraction.

MARGARET: Oh my God, look at that: a dead rat floating by.

MAN: For the pious Hindu, the city has always had a special meaning. Besides being a pilgrimage center, it is considered especially auspicious to die here, insuring an instant routing to heaven.

MARGARET: Oh my God, what's that?

GANESHA: Cow!

MARGARET: What's he saying?

GANESHA: Cow!

MARGARET: It looks like a cow.

MAN: I think it is.

GANESHA: Cow!

MARGARET: What's the Hindi word for "cow"?

MAN: I don't know.

MARGARET: I'm going to be sick.

KATHARINE: Tell us about the ghats, Mr. Tennyson.

MAN: Ghats are the steps which lead down to the river, from which pilgrims make their sin-cleansing dip in the Ganges. Dawn is the best time to visit them.

MARGARET: Oh my God, Kitty, look! It's a body.

KATHARINE: I see it, Margaret.

MAN: The pilgrims will be there for their early morning dip, the city will just be coming to life, the light is magical.

MARGARET: We're going to bump right into it!

(We hear the thud of the body against the skiff)

MAN: There are one hundred ghats in all, of which—

KATHARINE: Tell us about the burning ghats.

MAN: There are two principal ones, the Marnikarnika and the
Charanpaduka. There, you can just see the fires. This is where
bodies are cremated after making the final journey to the holy
Ganges —the men swathed in white cloth, the women in red— and
carried on a bamboo stretcher—or even the roof of a taxi.

GANESHA: Baby!

MARGARET: Oh my God, don't look, Kitty. It's a child.

GANESHA: Baby!

KATHARINE: Can you tell what sex it is?

MAN: Keep going, keep going!

GANESHA: Baby!

MARGARET: We're going to hit again! *(again we hear the sound of the
body hitting against the side of the skiff)* Oh, that sound!

GANESHA *(taking the skiff pole and poking at the body)*: Boy baby!

KATHARINE: It's a little boy.

MARGARET: How can you look even?!

MAN: Perhaps we should go back. Mrs. Civil doesn't seem able to
handle this.

MARGARET: You're right, she's not. Please, Kitty, I've had enough.

MAN *(to GANESHA)*: Back! Take us back!

(GANESHA *takes pole from the body and resumes navigating the skiff. In so doing, he splashes some water on* MARGARET)

MARGARET: Oh! Be careful! (MARGARET *is brushing at the water on her clothes*) He was poking that body with his pole! I feel slimy now.

KATHARINE: What brought you here, Mr. Tennyson?

MAN: It's Norman, please! I was looking for something I couldn't find in Wilkes-Barre, Pennsylvania. I forget what it was now but for a couple of minutes, back there in my youth, I thought I'd found it. Maybe it was just extra-good grass.

(*The sound of another body against the skiff*)

MARGARET: Please, can we get home?

KATHARINE: I thought I would be more appalled by all this.

MAN: Thought or hoped? Some people come to Varanasi to find their hearts have completely hardened. It's a terrible realization.

MARGARET: What are we supposed to do? I can't accept all this. My heart and mind would break if I did. And yet I must. I know it.

KATHARINE: Everything in and on this river seems inevitable and right. Something dead, floating there.

MARGARET: It's a dog.

KATHARINE: That old woman with the sagging breasts bathing herself oblivious to us.

MARGARET: She's lovely.

KATHARINE: Even us in our Burberry raincoats. We all have a place here. Nothing is right, nothing is wrong. Allow. Accept. Be.

MARGARET: Yes.

(MAN *brings skiff to shore. He leaps off and helps the others to disembark*)

MAN: Home again. I think you'll find the shopping here a little more to your liking. Varanasi is famous all over India for silk brocade.

KATHARINE: I'm still looking for a figure of Ganesh.

MARGARET: You've already bought almost a dozen.

KATHARINE: I'm looking for a perfect Ganesh.

MAN: Is there such a thing?

KATHARINE: I'm sure of it.

MAN: Let's get a move on, ladies. We have Sarnath before lunch.

MARGARET: What's in Sarnath?

MAN: Buddha!

(*They walk away from* GANESHA, *who looks after them, brings his hands together and bows*)

GANESHA: You're welcome. You're welcome. You're welcome.

(*He has* MARGARET'*s binoculars,* KATHARINE'*s first Ganesh figure and the* MAN'*s Marlboros.*

Lights are changing.)

Scene Five

A hotel room. There are louvred doors leading to a balcony fronting on a street.

KATHARINE: May I? (MARGARET *stands with her back to us. She holds her blouse open to* KATHARINE *who is sitting in front of her. A dog is barking off. It stops. In the silence*) Oh!

MARGARET (*closing her blouse and beginning to button it*): I don't know what annoys me more about this country: the heat, the music or the barking dogs.

KATHARINE: How long have you known?

MARGARET: I wasn't sure until that first night in Bombay.

KATHARINE: We'll go back at once.

MARGARET: No, we've come this far, I want to see the Taj Mahal. It's just a few more days.

KATHARINE: But you promise you'll—?

MARGARET: Of course.

KATHARINE: Just as soon as we get back!

MARGARET: Absolutely.

KATHARINE: I'm so sorry, Margaret.

MARGARET: Well. And that's about as philosophical as I'm going to get. I don't want anyone else to know; unless I have to, of course.

KATHARINE: Of course not. Thank you for confiding in me. It means a good deal to me. More than you could know. I need a friend. That sounds ridiculous at my age. But you're going to tell Alan, of course?

MARGARET: I don't know. Not if I don't have to. It would give him one more reason to work late. He's had one reason for almost seven years. Her name is DeKennesey. She must be divorced. I know she's got two kids. I've seen them. She's only ten years younger than me. He's got her in one of those condos by the club.

KATHARINE: I had no idea.

MARGARET: We're not supposed to.

KATHARINE: I'm so sorry.

MARGARET: You've got to stop saying that. What happens to women? Who are we? What are we supposed to do? What are we supposed to be? Men still have all the marbles. All we have are our children and sooner or later we lose them. (*She goes to the louvred doors, opens them and goes out. Lights up on* MAN. *He is a leper, as hideous as the first one*) Your friend is back down there.

KATHARINE: You think I'm crazy, don't you?

MARGARET: Yes.

(KATHARINE *has joined* MARGARET *on the balcony looking down at the* MAN)

KATHARINE: I couldn't do it. Yesterday, while you were resting, I went down to the lobby and ordered tea and just sat and stared at him out there. I felt so drawn to him, Margaret, yet so repulsed. I had to go out to him.

(*She moves out of the room and to the* MAN. MARGARET *stays on the balcony watching them*)

MARGARET: I was up here. I wanted to call out to you but I didn't. I guess I wanted you to do it for the both of us.

KATHARINE: Why are you diseased and hideous? What can I do to change that?

MAN: Love me.

(Lights up on GANESHA, *again with his elephant's head)*

GANESHA: Love me, the man said and smiled at the lovely American.

KATHARINE: Here, in the warmth and light of India, I want to hold you in my arms, as I could not hold my son while he lay dying on a dark city street.

MAN: Love me.

GANESHA: Love me, the man said again and smiled again.

KATHARINE: Now, in this moment when we are so close but so alone, I want to kiss you on the lips, as I could never kiss my son for fear of terrifying him over how much I loved him.

MAN: Love me.

GANESHA: Love me, the man said again but this time he did not smile.

KATHARINE: You frighten me. You disgust me.

MAN: Love me.

KATHARINE: I cannot do it.

GANESHA: And Mrs. Katharine Brynne reached into her purse and gave the man fifty rupees and one of her perfect Ganeshas. She did not sleep well that night. She worried about her soul. The man, however, had the finest meal of his entire, miserable life.

*(*KATHARINE *comes back to* MARGARET *on the balcony. Again they look down at the* MAN *just sitting there)*

MARGARET: I couldn't do it either.

KATHARINE: The whole trip was a failure then.

MARGARET: You're too hard on yourself. You can't save the world.

KATHARINE: I can't even save myself. Here.

(She hands MARGARET *another of her Ganeshas)*

MARGARET: That's one of your favorites.

KATHARINE: There's plenty more where it came from. I've got more than a dozen of them now. I still haven't found the perfect one.

GANESHA: They're all perfect, Katharine.

(With a gesture he reveals a dazzling array of all sorts of Ganeshas: stone, clay, ivory, etc.

KATHARINE: I know. I wish I could believe that. I can't. I just can't. *(To* MARGARET*)* It's for good luck with—.

MARGARET: You're a kind woman.

(They just look at each other a moment. It would be hard to say who opens her arms to the other first. They embrace. They kiss)

KATHARINE: The Taj Mahal, then home.

MARGARET: The Taj Mahal!

(Light change.

Blinding light. It should be hard to look at the stage.

Music.)

Scene Six

The Taj Mahal. We see it through MARGARET *and* KATHARINE's *eyes. They are transfixed.*

GANESHA: What does one say before such beauty? If one is wise, very, very little.

(The MAN *appears. He is another* AMERICAN TOURIST *reading from a guidebook)*

MAN: If there's a building which evokes a country —like the Eiffel Tower does for France, the Sydney Opera House for Australia— then it has to be the Taj Mahal for India.

MARGARET: Do you mind? We're trying to appreciate all this.

MAN: It's a free country.

KATHARINE: No, that's America. This is India.

(He withdraws. The two women are in rapture)

MARGARET: I've stopped breathing.

KATHARINE: My heart is pounding.

MARGARET: This has been worth everything.

KATHARINE: It's the most beautiful thing I've ever seen.

MARGARET: I'm not going to cry. I refuse to cry.

KATHARINE: Go right ahead. I just may join you.

MARGARET: Do you think this is why we exist? To create this?

KATHARINE: I don't know. I don't think I can talk.

MARGARET: I think it's better maybe if we don't.

KATHARINE: I want you to see what I'm seeing. Look, over there!

MARGARET: I see it, I see it. And over there, Kitty, have you ever . . . ?

KATHARINE: We're in paradise. This is a dream. It isn't true.

MARGARET: But it is true. And we're here. And we will have this forever.

KATHARINE: Look!

MARGARET: Look!

(GANESHA *draws a filmy gauze drape across the stage. It is the first time the stage has been "closed" the entire evening*)

GANESH: Two days later, they were back in Connecticut, met at the airport by a solemn delegation of Alan Civil and various Brynnes bearing the mournful news of Katharine's husband, the glare ice and the oak tree. Vacations can end abruptly like this. Trips have a way of going on. Mrs. Civil and Mrs. Brynne's visit to India was of the second variety.

(He pulls back the gauze curtain. To one side is a king-size bed. KATHA-RINE *is undressing to get into it. On the other side, there are twin beds.* MARGARET *is getting ready to get into one of them. The* MAN *is already in his bed. He is* ALAN*)*

MARGARET: What's this postcard? *(She picks up a postcard on the pillow)*

MAN: It came yesterday. It was addressed to the two of you. What were you two doing over there? Picking up strange men? That was a joke, Margaret. (MARGARET *sits on the edge of the bed and reads the card*) I'll never know if we did the right thing. But who knew where to find you? It's a big country. I said to their kids, go to the Taj Mahal, hang out, sooner or later, they'll turn up. Everybody thought I was kidding. I thought it was a good idea. Good night, Margaret. I'm glad you're home. I missed you.

(He turns out the light. MARGARET *picks up the phone and dials a number.* KATHARINE *is sitting on the edge of her bed. She is humming/ singing "Blow the Wind Southerly." The telephone rings)*

KATHARINE: Yes?

MARGARET: Are you okay?

KATHARINE: Better than expected.

MARGARET: We got a postcard from Harry and Ben.

KATHARINE: I'm sorry, I don't—.

MARGARET: Yes, you do! The two young men, next door, our first day in Bombay. They were both sick.

KATHARINE: I remember.

MARGARET: "Dear Girls, (all right, *ladies!*), welcome home! Hope you had a wonderful trip and didn't have to use that police whistle again. Did you see the Taj Mahal? Didn't you die just a little? Thanks for all your kindness. Harry is still in the hospital here but doing well. We're both hanging in there. What else are you gonna do? Love, Ben." Guess who the postcard's of? Your favorite, Ganesha. A perfect Ganesh. I'll bring it over tomorrow. Are you sure you're okay?

KATHARINE: I'm fine.

MARGARET: I love you.

KATHARINE: Thank you.

MARGARET: You're supposed to say "I love you, too."

KATHARINE: I love you, too, Margaret.

MARGARET: Good night, Kitty.

KATHARINE: Good night.

(They hang up. They each are sitting on the edge of their beds. KATHA-
RINE *begins to sing/hum "Blow The Wind Southerly." The* MAN *has
begun to snore.* MARGARET *looks at him, then at the postcard and begins
to sing/hum "Swing Low, Sweet Chariot." At exactly the same time,
the two women get into bed and under the covers.* GANESHA *appears
between them. He takes off his elephant's head. His face is gilded and
he is revealed as a handsome man. He bends over* MARGARET *and kisses
her. She stops singing and sleeps. Then he bends over* KATHARINE *and
kisses her. She, too, stops singing and sleeps. The* MAN *is still snoring)*

GANESHA *(singing)*:
  "Good night, ladies
  Good night, ladies
  Good night, ladies
  The milkman's on his way."
  *(He pulls the drape across the stage. He looks at us. He puts his
  finger to his lips)* Goodnight. *(He disappears through the curtain.
  The* MAN *is still snoring at the end of the play.)*